hello.

Welcome to the new edition of my magazine!
It's full of fun and healthy recipes for all the
family during the cold winter months

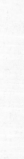

Autumn and winter are eventful seasons, with Hallowe'en, Bonfire Night and Christmas just a few of the major events being celebrated – and what good is a celebration without scrummy food for all the family?

In this Winter & Christmas issue, I take you on a culinary journey, from fresh baby purées through to foods from around the world – it's good to introduce different flavours to children from an early age.

Also take a look at my healthy lunchbox options – I've created them to be high in taste and low in effort, which is crucial for busy parents. And speaking of healthiness, Dr Adam Fox explains what you need to know about allergies on p8.

I've always believed that cooking and eating should be a fun and engaging process, and that's why I think you'll really enjoy the ghoulish recipes and games in the Hallowe'en section and the creative Christmas treats in the final chapter.

I hope you enjoy these recipes – I'll be bringing you more in spring and summer!

Annabel Karmel

On seeing the bigger picture

THERE ARE MANY SOURCES OF ENERGY, BUT NOT ONE OF THEM IS THE SOLUTION.

THERE ARE MANY SOURCES OF ENERGY, AND THAT IS THE SOLUTION.

145

Annabel Karmel Family Cookbook

contents

❀ **Allergies** 08
Allergy specialist Dr Adam Fox shows you
how to spot allergies in children and what
you need to know about them

✎ **Baby Purées** 16
Treat your curious bundle of joy to their
first tastes of real food with these delicious
and healthy purées

🐾 **World Animal Day** 30
Celebrate World Animal Day by creating
cute versions of your pets. Decorating food
has never been so much fun

🐻 **Toddlers** 48
Match your child's growing appetite with
healthy homemade versions of children's
favourites, such as beefburgers

🍎 **Lunchboxes** 64
Stress-free sandwich and lunchbox ideas
to keep your tiny tearaways fully charged
during school time

♡ **Kids love cooking** 78
Spend quality time with your children and
encourage them to learn the basics of cooking
– they'll love getting their hands dirty!

🦇 **Hallowe'en** 92
Host the best ever Hallowe'en party with
fancy dress, party games and, of course,
some wonderfully ghoulish recipes

🔥 **Bonfire Night** 110
A selection of warming recipes that will
keep everyone's fire glowing on a chilly
winter evening

🌍 **World Food** 122
Take your child's tastebuds on a world
tour to discover the deliciously different
flavours on offer

★ **Christmas** 140
Who said Christmas menus have to be the
same every year? Use these fun recipes to
make the festive season one to remember

■ **Competition** 162

recipes

155

136

21

🥄 Baby Purées

Trio of Root Vegetables 21
Apple, Blueberry and Pear 22
Mashed Potato, Sweet Potato and Broccoli 24
Carrot Purée With Tomato, Basil
and Cheese 25
Tasty Fish with Sweet Potato 26
Hidden-Vegetable Bolognese 27
Chicken With Sweet Potato and Apricot 28
Lovely Lentils 29

🐾 World Animal Day

Buzzy Bees 33
Poodle Party Cake 35
Mice in Jackets 40
Cucumber Crocodile 41
Cheesy Bread Animals 43
Bagel Snake 44
Chocolate Teddy Bear Cupcakes 44
Annabel's Mini Fish Pie 47

🐻 Toddlers

Chinese-Style Rice With Chicken
and Prawns 52
Crispy Sweet-Chilli Chicken Fingers 55
Chicken and Corn Chowder 55
Funny Face Beefburgers 57
Toasted Tuna Muffin 58
Tasty Salmon Balls 59
Baked Macaroni Cheese with Ham
and Tomato 61
Vegetarian Shepherd's Pie 63

🍎 Lunchboxes

Top 10 Sandwich Fillings 68
Kiddie Sushi-style Roll 69
Lara's Chicken Wraps 71
Prawn and Avocado Wrap 71
Turkey Wrap With Plum Sauce 71
Homemade Tomato Soup 72
Mummy's Minestrone Soup 73
Bagels With Smoked Salmon/Cream Cheese,
Ham/Cheese, Tomato/Mozzarella/Basil 74
Annabel's Apricot Cookies 77

♡ Kids Love Cooking

Easy Cupcakes 82
Marshmallow Sheep Cupcakes 82
Pink Piggy Cupcakes 83
Puppy Dog Cupcakes 83
Sweetcorn Fritters 84
Multi-Coloured Meringues 86
Apple Smiles 88
Peanut-Butter Bears 89
Shortbread Sweethearts 90

🦇 Hallowe'en

Scary Monster Cupcakes 99
Brain Cupcakes 100
Ghoulish Ghost Cakes 100
Bat and Ghost Cookies 103
Chocolate Spider Cakes 105
Twiglet Broomsticks 106
Deadman's Finger Sandwiches 107
Pumpkin Oranges 108
Green Slime Lemonade 108

🔥 Bonfire Night

Stuffed Baked Potatoes 114
Baby Baked Potatoes 115
Stuffed Sweet Potatoes With Bacon 116
Beefy Sausage Rolls 117
Sesame Honey Drumsticks 119
Sticky Drumsticks 119
Nachos With Salsa 119
Sausage Rockets 120
Toffee Apples 121

🌏 World Food

Sesame Beef Stir-Fry 125

Fruity Chicken Curry 127

Moneybag Wontons Dim Sum 128

Chicken and Prawn Dumplings Dim Sum 128

Corn and Chicken Laksa 131

Teryaki Salmon and Easy Chinese
Fried Rice 132

Annabel's Thai Chicken Soup 134

Singapore Noodles 135

Annabel's Paella 136

Chicken Fajitas 138

★ Christmas

Stained-Glass Window Cookies 145

Ginger and Spice Snowflake Cookies 147

Annabel's Granola 148

Peppermint and Rose Kisses 151

White Chocolate and Cranberry Cookies 153

Snazzy Snowmen 154

Father Christmas Carrot Cupcakes 155

Christmas Pudding Truffles 157

Annabel's Turkey Meatballs and Spaghetti 158

Rudolph the Red-Nosed Baked Potato .. 159

Mini Turkey and Potato Pies 161

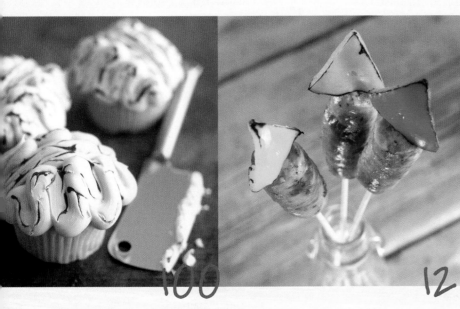

Annabel Karmel
🍎 Family Cookbook

ART & DESIGN

ART EDITORS Sarah Bridges, Nick Watts

PHOTOGRAPHY Dave King

FOOD STYLIST Seiko Hatfield

PROPS STYLIST Jo Harris

MAKE-UP STYLIST Liz Beckett

REPRO Linda Duong

EDITORIAL

SUB EDITORS Nicola Tann, Jo Halpin

THANKS TO Rose Catt, Graham Foster

ADVERTISING

ADVERTISING DIRECTOR Sophie Kochan 020 7907 6741

MARKETING Michelle Marsh

MANAGEMENT

BOOKAZINE MANAGER Dharmesh Mistry
(020 7907 6100 dharmesh_mistry@dennis.co.uk)

PRODUCTION DIRECTOR Robin Ryan

GROUP ADVERTISING DIRECTOR Julian Lloyd-Evans

NEWSTRADE DIRECTOR Martin Belson

CHIEF OPERATING OFFICER Brett Reynolds

GROUP FINANCE DIRECTOR Ian Leggett

CHIEF EXECUTIVE James Tye

CHAIRMAN Felix Dennis

A DENNIS PUBLICATION

Dennis Publishing, 30 Cleveland St, London W1T 4JD.
Company registered in England.
Text © Annabel Karmel & Dennis Publishing Limited; photography
© Dave King, DK & Ebury Press. Licensed by Felden 2009, and may
not be reproduced in whole or part without the consent
of the publishers. The "Magbook" brand is a trademark of Dennis
Publishing Ltd. Dennis Publishing operates an efficient commercial
reprints service. For more details please call 020 7907 6100

Printed at BGP
The paper used within this bookazine is produced from sustainable
fibre, manufactured by mills with a valid chain of custody.

Food Allergies
in babies and children

Food allergies among young children are becoming more commonplace. Here, allergy specialist Dr Adam Fox explains what you need to know about them

Dr Adam Fox – Consultant Paediatric Allergist
www.adamfox.co.uk

Food allergies in babies and children

Almost one in 12 young children suffers from a food allergy, which seem to be getting more and more common. But what are food allergies, would you recognise if your child had one and what could you do about it?

■ What is a food allergy?

The past 40 years have seen a dramatic rise in allergic diseases such as asthma, eczema and hayfever, particularly in the Western world. Along with this 'allergy epidemic' has come an increase in food allergies. Once a medical curiosity, now almost every classroom in the US, UK and Australia has a child who has to avoid milk, egg or nuts.

Food allergies occur when your immune system becomes confused – instead of ignoring harmless food proteins, it triggers a reaction that leads to the release of a chemical called histamine. It is this that causes the classic allergy symptoms of hives or swelling. If the reaction becomes severe, it is called anaphylaxis and this type of reaction may be life-threatening.

Scientists are still puzzled as to why there has been such a rapid increase in allergies. The most popular explanation is the 'hygiene hypothesis', which suggests the increasing cleanliness of the modern world is leaving our immune systems under-stimulated. With too few bacteria and viruses to fight, our

Food allergies in different parts of the world

Worldwide milk, egg
USA, UK, Australia peanut and tree nuts
France mustard seed
Italy, Spain peach, apple, shellfish
Israel sesame
Spain, Japan fish
Japan buckwheat
Singapore bird's nest, shellfish

body's defences start to direct inappropriate responses towards harmless things such as pollen or foods. Indeed, as parts of the developing world become more Westernised, doctors are noticing an increase in allergy sufferers there, too.

Most serious food allergies start in infancy and early childhood. They are caused by a relatively small number of different foods.

and tend to disappear by themselves during childhood. Other common food 'allergens' vary depending on where you live. While peanut and tree-nut allergies are common in the US, UK and Australia, fish and seafood allergies are more common in South-East Asia and Southern Europe. Other common problem foods include wheat, soy, sesame and kiwi.

How will I know if my baby has a food allergy?

Food allergies are far more common among children in families where other members suffer from an allergy. Babies who suffer from eczema are particularly at risk of food allergies. The more severe the eczema, and the earlier in life it began, the more likely there is to be a food allergy. A baby younger than three months suffering with severe eczema is very likely to suffer from food allergies.

Some food allergies are quite easy to spot – as soon as the food is eaten (often for the first or second time) an itchy rash develops, usually around the mouth. There may also be swelling of the face, runny nose and itchiness, as well as vomiting. With severe reactions, there may be difficulty breathing and, if this occurs, you should call an ambulance immediately. Fortunately, these kinds of severe reactions are very rare in young children and tend to be more of a problem among teenagers.

Symptoms of an immediate allergic reaction

Mild to moderate symptoms typically affect the skin, the respiratory system and the gut

- A flushed face, hives, a red and itchy rash around the mouth, tongue or eyes. This can spread across the entire body
- Mild swelling, particularly of the lips, eyes and face
- A runny or blocked nose, sneezing and watery eyes
- Nausea and vomiting, tummy cramps and diarrhoea
- A scratchy or itchy mouth and throat

Severe symptoms (anaphylaxis). These require urgent medical attention

- Wheezing or tightness in the chest, similar to an asthma attack
- Swelling of the tongue and throat, restricting the airways This can cause noisy breathing (especially breathing in), a cough or a change in voice
- A sudden drop in blood pressure (called hypertension) leading to shock
- Dizziness, confusion, collapse, loss of consciousness and sometimes coma

"Babies who suffer from eczema are particularly at risk of food allergies"

Symptoms of a delayed allergic reaction

- Eczema
- Reflux (an effortless vomiting)
- Poor growth
- Swelling in the small bowel
- Constipation and/or diarrhoea
- Raising knees to chest with tummy pain
- Frequent distress and crying

Sometimes, food allergies can be more subtle and difficult to detect, especially if they are delayed allergies. These tend to be more of a problem in infancy. In the past, these allergies were sometimes called food intolerance, but this isn't the correct term because an intolerance doesn't involve the immune system. Delayed allergic reactions do involve the immune system, but – unlike the histamine-release characteristic of an immediate reaction – delayed allergies involve parts of the immune system that take much longer to respond. The end result means it's difficult to pinpoint a particular food as the problem and sufferers may continue to eat or drink the food allergen. Delayed allergies in infants may cause chronic symptoms such as eczema, reflux, colic, poor growth, diarrhoea or even constipation. The symptoms only get better when the food is removed from the diet, with milk, soy, egg and wheat being the most common culprits. However, all of these symptoms commonly occur during childhood and an allergic reaction is only one possible explanation – and not the only one. Trying to work out whether the problem is a food allergy can be very difficult and requires the help of an experienced doctor.

Working out whether the problem is a food allergy requires the help of an experienced doctor

"Being diagnosed
with a food allergy
has a massive impact
on the whole family"

▪ What should I do if I suspect an allergy?

Immediate allergies to food are usually quite easy to spot because of how quickly they happen after the food is eaten. If you think your child has had an immediate reaction, it is best to avoid the food until you have seen a doctor. If you suspect something in your child's diet is causing more delayed symptoms – such as eczema or reflux – it can be helpful to keep a food diary to see if the relationship between having the food in the diet (or in your diet if you are breastfeeding) and the symptoms are consistent. If they are, the diary will be helpful to the doctor to whom you take your child.

▪ What can my doctor do for me?

Diagnosing food allergies relies on keeping a careful medical history, examination and special allergy tests. Your doctor will ask you about the symptoms of the reaction, whether they have happened every time the food has been eaten and how long they took to appear. With immediate allergies, testing can be done by a blood test or by a 'skin-prick' test, when food extracts are placed on the skin of the arm. Either test can be very helpful in confirming if the allergy is present. Unfortunately, things are less easy with delayed allergies because there are not any reliable and straightforward tests. However, careful exclusion diets – with the suspected food completely taken out of the diet – may be recommended with the assistance of an experienced dietician. If the food is the cause of the symptoms, these should improve when the food is withdrawn. This exclusion period should be followed by reintroduction of the food to ensure any improvement was due to its removal. If the symptoms are relieved on exclusion, but return on reintroduction, a diagnosis can be reached.

▪ Looking after a child with a food allergy

The best treatment for a food allergy is to completely avoid the problem food. Being diagnosed with a food allergy has a massive impact on the whole family. Eating is such a central part of daily life that having to be absolutely sure a child has no contact with a particular food affects mealtimes, going to school, holidays and social occasions. A simple supermarket trip has been shown to be almost 40% longer when shopping for a food-allergic child. Parents also need to be able to recognise reactions and know exactly how to deal with them when they occur. This usually involves carrying antihistamines everywhere the child goes and, for those children at risk of anaphylaxis, adrenaline injections as well. Children with food allergies are also at risk of missing out on essential nutrients they would get from the food they are avoiding, especially in the case of infants with a milk allergy. Fortunately, there are now many specially designed milk substitutes and, with the help of a dietician, a nutritious diet can be achieved, even for children with multiple food allergies.

Many food allergies, such as egg and milk, are outgrown during childhood, while allergies to peanuts, nuts, fish and shellfish tend not to go away. Children with food allergies also have a high chance of other allergic problems, such as asthma, eczema and hayfever. It is essential children with food allergies continue to be seen by their doctors as they grow up. Repeating allergy tests can help to predict if the allergy has been outgrown, so the food can be carefully reintroduced into the diet. It is also essential the child be examined for any signs they are missing out on essential nutrients because of their restricted diet or that they are developing signs of other allergic problems. ✿

Unfortunately, there appears to be no cure for food allergies on the horizon, although exciting research does promise real progress over the next five to 10 years, not only in our understanding of how to prevent allergies in the first place, but in helping those who already have them

Substituting foods

In my *Fussy Eaters' Recipe Book*, there's a whole chapter of gluten-free recipes. You can substitute wheat-free and gluten-free flours in many of my recipes, but there are always some that just don't work. It is generally best to substitute when there is a low ratio of flour to other ingredients, as you are less reliant on the gluten to hold the mixture together. Use well-greased non-stick tins because gluten-free goods are always a little fragile.

Dairy

Dairy provides protein, fat, carbohydrate and vitamin D as well as being rich in calcium – essential for strong bones and teeth

Good substitutes

Soya milk, soya yoghurts, soya cream

Rice milk, oat milk, coconut milk

Dairy-free cheeses

Margarine (but check the label as some contain milk)

Non-dairy ice cream

Other calcium-rich foods

Leafy vegetables

Wholegrain bread

Pulses

Dried fruit

Nuts and seeds

Tinned sardines and salmon

Wheat

Good substitutes

Gluten-free flour

Xanthan gum acts as a gluten substitute, adding springiness to bread and helping to hold together gluten-free pastry that would otherwise crumble

Rice cakes

Rice noodles

Buckwheat noodles

Rice

Corn millet cereals

Polenta

Quinoa

Buckwheat

Millet

Cornflour and arrowroot are good thickeners

Sources of fibre

Good substitutes

Fibre-rich pulses

Brown rice

Seeds and nuts

Dried fruits

Fresh fruit and vegetables

Nuts

Although nuts are not essential to the diet, they are a valuable source of protein for vegetarians. Vegetarians with a nut allergy should eat protein rich pulses eg: lentils, eggs, cheese and other dairy products

Good substitutes (if not allergic to them)

Pine nuts and seeds

Eggs

Good source of protein and vitamins and used to make cakes and cookies

Good substitutes

You can buy egg-replacer powders for baking cakes and cookies

Egg-free mayonnaise

Tofu can add an eggy texture to food

The Perfect Lemon Polenta Cake

■ Serves 10   ■ Prep time: 10 mins   ■ Cook time: 50 mins

450g/16oz unsalted butter, softened

450g/16oz caster sugar

450g/16oz ground almonds

2 tbsp vanilla extract

6 eggs

Grated zest of 4 lemons

Juice of 1 lemon

225g/8oz polenta

1 tbsp baking powder

½ tbsp salt

Gluten-free flour for dusting

Preheat the oven to 160C/300F/Gas Mark 3. Butter and flour a 30cm (12in) round cake tin. Using an electric mixer, beat the butter and sugar together until pale and light. Stir in the ground almonds and vanilla. Beat in the eggs, one at a time. Fold in the lemon zest and juice, polenta, baking powder and salt. Spoon into the prepared tin and bake for about 45 minutes or until set. The cake will be brown on top.

As food intolerances become more common, many people are looking for **wheat-free** recipes. This cake is **divine** and certainly **too good to miss** – even if you don't have to avoid wheat...

warming
and wonderful
baby food

It's amazing how far your baby has come.
In just six months, your tiny helpless
newborn has grown into a
beaming bundle of curiosity ready
to enjoy their first taste of real food

Warming and wonderful baby food

This is such an exciting stage. Guiding your baby through their first meals is a learning experience for both of you.

Simple homemade fruit, vegetable and rice purées are ideal for your little one's first tastes. Those first meals are about understanding what to do with an advancing spoon, experiencing different flavours and soft textures, and learning to swallow food.

Once you've got the hang of mealtimes, it's time to try out different tastes. Enjoying new flavours now might help your baby be less fussy later on. And, of course, your growing baby increasingly needs the energy and nutrients that only good fresh food can provide. Try my Trio of Root Vegetables (p21) followed by Apple, Blueberry and Pear Purée (p22) for an all-natural vitamin-packed meal.

There's something indescribably sweet about a baby's reaction to new tastes, whether it's a positive 'yum' or a definite 'yuk!'. It shows your baby is developing their own personality and definite opinions.

As your active baby develops, they'll really benefit from the calories that foods like cheese and avocado provide, as babies grow more rapidly in their first year than at any other time and need calories to fuel their rapid growth. It's also important to introduce red meat, because a baby's store of iron runs out at six months, as well as oily fish, such as salmon, because their essential fatty acids are very important for brain development. They'll find varied flavours increasingly rewarding and 'chewing' with their gums satisfying. Tasty Carrot Purée with Tomato, Basil and Cheese (p25) or Chicken with Sweet Potato and Apricot (p28) are perfect for healthy young appetites.

Food is so much more than nourishment of course – it's at the heart of family life. And now your baby is on solids, you can enjoy eating together. Everyone will like Hidden Vegetable Bolognese (p27) – simply mash up your baby's portion and sit down together for your first real family meal.

The Annabel Karmel & Lindam weaning range is an innovative and practical set that will help babies progress from first tastes to feeding themselves.

The 10-piece weaning set includes a mess mat, bib, feeding spoon, non-spill cup, small bowl, cutlery case, large bowl with finger food tray, and a spoon and 'foon'. This stylish, stain proof range comes in bright red.

Available from Waitrose, John Lewis, Ocado, Asda, Amazon.co.uk, Kiddicare, Findel Education, Bump to 3 and Mothercare

Trio of Root Vegetables

- Age 6 months+ ■ Makes 4 portions
- Prep time: 8 mins ■ Cook time: 17 mins
- Suitable for freezing

200g/7oz carrots, peeled and chopped
100g/4oz parsnip, peeled and chopped
200g/7oz sweet potato, peeled and chopped
A small knob of butter

Steam the carrots and parsnip for five minutes. Add the sweet potato and continue to steam for 10 to 12 minutes or until the vegetables are tender. Blend to a purée with the knob of butter. Add a bit of your baby's usual milk if the mixture is too thick.

Root-vegetable purées are great for babies. Sweet potato is full of **protective** antioxidants, including betacarotene, vitamin C and vitamin E, that **boost the immune system**

Orange fruits and vegetables tend to be rich in **betacarotene**, which is **essential** for **growth and good vision**

Blueberries have the highest antioxidant content of any fruit. Little fruits that are big on taste and nutrients, blueberries are packed with vitamin C, which can help reduce the severity and duration of colds and flu

Apple, Blueberry and Pear

- Age 6 months+   - Makes 5 portions
- Prep time: 6 mins   - Cook time: 7 mins
- Suitable for freezing

2 sweet eating apples, peeled, cored and chopped
75g/3oz blueberries
2 ripe pears, peeled, cored and chopped

Put the apple and pear into a heavy-based saucepan and cook, covered, for three minutes. Add the blueberries, cover and cook for three more minutes. Remove the cover and cook for one more minute. Blend to a purée. You could also add some mashed banana or stir in some yoghurt.

Vitamin C is also needed for growth and skin repair, and plays an important role in protecting the heart and preventing cancers. It also helps us absorb iron

Try adding mashed banana or yoghurt

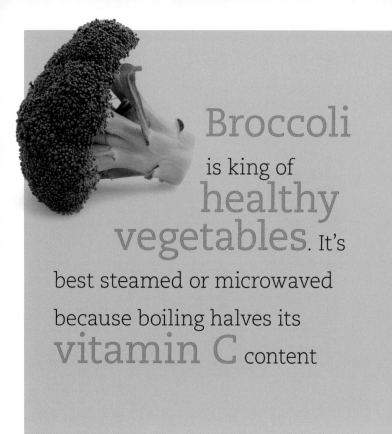

Broccoli

is king of **healthy vegetables**. It's best steamed or microwaved because boiling halves its **vitamin C** content

Mashed Potato, Sweet Potato and Broccoli

- Age 8 months+ ■ Makes 3 portions
- Prep time: 7 mins ■ Cook time: 12 mins
- Suitable for freezing

150g/6oz potato, peeled and chopped
200g/7oz sweet potato, peeled and chopped
60g/2oz broccoli florets
4 tbsp milk
40g/2oz grated mature Cheddar cheese
Generous knob of butter

Put the potato and sweet potato in a saucepan, cover with boiling water and cook for about 12 minutes, until tender. Meanwhile, either steam the broccoli until tender (about five minutes) or microwave it in a dish with five tablespoons of water for about four minutes. Drain the potato and sweet potato, and mash together with the broccoli, knob of butter, milk and grated cheese.

sweet potato combines well with fruit such as apples

If your baby isn't keen on green vegetables, it's a good idea to mix them with **sweet-tasting root vegetables** such as sweet potato

carrot Purée with Tomato, Basil and cheese

- Age 6 months+
- Makes 5 portions
- Prep time: 8 mins
- Cook time: 18 mins
- Suitable for freezing

2 large carrots, peeled and sliced
60g/2oz of cauliflower florets
Generous knob of butter
3 tomatoes, skinned, deseeded and roughly chopped
75g/3oz cheddar cheese
Fresh basil leaves

Steam the carrots for 12 minutes. Add the cauliflower and continue to cook for about six minutes. Meanwhile, melt the knob of butter and sauté the tomatoes for about two minutes or until slightly mushy. Stir in the grated cheese until melted. Tear two basil leaves into pieces and add to the tomato sauce. Blend the vegetables with the cheese and tomato sauce. Alternatively, mash the vegetables together with the cheese and tomato sauce.

Tasty Fish with Sweet Potato

- Age 6 months+ ■ Makes 3 portions
- Prep time: 10 mins ■ Cook time: 12 mins
- Suitable for freezing

275g/9oz sweet potato, peeled and chopped
2 ripe tomatoes, skinned, deseeded and chopped
Generous knob of butter
40g/2oz cheddar cheese, grated
150g/6oz plaice fillets, skinned
2 tbsp milk

Steam the sweet potato for about 10 minutes or until tender.
Meanwhile, score a cross in the base of the tomatoes and plunge
into boiling water for about 30 seconds. Transfer to ice-cold
water and the skins should peel off easily. Deseed and roughly
chop the tomatoes. Melt the knob of butter in a saucepan and
sauté the tomatoes for about two minutes until mushy. Remove
from the heat and stir in the grated cheese until melted.
Put the plaice fillets into a microwave dish, add the milk and dot
with butter. Cover, leaving the vent open, and cook for one and a
half minutes on full power.

   Drain the cooked fish and flake carefully to check there are
no bones. Add to the tomato and cheese sauce, together with the
cooking liquid from the fish. Add the cooked sweet potato and
mash together.

This is a tasty recipe for introducing your baby to fish – plaice is one of the best types to start with because it has a lovely soft texture. If fish is overcooked, it becomes dry and tasteless – one of the best ways of cooking fish is in the microwave

Try my micro steam oval bowls with valves in the lid, designed for microwaving fish and vegetables for your baby. Cooking in a microwave is a good way to preserve nutrients

Add seasoning for a tasty family meal

Hidden-vegetable Bolognese

■ Age 6 months+ ■ Makes 4 portions ■ Prep time: 8 mins ■ Cook time: 30 mins ■ Suitable for freezing

1 tbsp olive oil

Half onion, finely chopped

40g/2oz leek, thinly sliced

¼ stick celery, diced

½ small courgette, chopped

1 small carrot, chopped

Half eating apple, peeled, cored and grated

1 clove garlic, crushed

200g/7oz tin chopped tomatoes

225g/8oz minced beef

1 tbsp tomato purée

1 tbsp tomato ketchup

175ml/6fl oz stock

¼ tsp dried oregano

100g mini shell pasta

Heat the oil in a large frying pan and sauté the vegetables, apple and garlic for 10 minutes, until soft. Transfer to a blender and add the tomatoes, then whizz until smooth.

Wipe the pan with a piece of kitchen paper and add the mince. Fry over a medium to high heat, breaking the mince up with a wooden spoon until browned. If your child likes a finer texture, transfer the browned mince to a food processor and whizz until well chopped.

Add the tomato and vegetable sauce to the mince then stir in the tomato purée, ketchup, stock and oregano. Bring to a simmer and cook for 15 minutes, until the sauce is thick. Season to taste with salt and pepper (for babies over one year).

Meanwhile, cook the pasta shells according to the instructions on the packet. Drain, mix with the bolognese sauce and serve.

If your child won't eat vegetables, bolognese is a good way to hide them

Sweet potato and apricots are a good source of betacarotene, which is essential for growth and fighting infection. Dried apricots are a real superfood. Drying increases their concentration of betacarotene, potassium and iron – but avoid buying dried apricots treated with sulphur dioxide

chicken with Sweet Potato and Apricot

- Age 6 months+ ■ Makes 4 portions
- Prep time: 8 mins ■ Cook time: 12 mins
- Suitable for freezing

2 tsp light olive oil
30g/1oz leek, finely sliced
85g/3oz chicken breast, cut into chunks
150g/6oz sweet potato (1 small sweet potato), peeled and chopped
3 dried apricots, chopped
250ml/8fl oz chicken stock or water

Heat the oil in a pan and sauté the leek for two to three minutes, stirring occasionally, until softened. Add the chicken and sauté for about two minutes until sealed. Add the sweet potato, chopped apricots and chicken stock. Bring to the boil, then cover and simmer for about 15 minutes. Allow to cool and then purée in a blender.

Lovely Lentils

- Age 6 months+ - Makes 6 portions
- Prep time: 8 mins - Cook time: 38 mins
- Suitable for freezing

1 tbp vegetable oil

50g/2oz chopped onion or leek

100g/4oz carrots, peeled and chopped

15g/½oz celery, chopped

50g/2oz split red lentils

250g/8oz sweet potato, peeled and chopped

200ml/7fl oz passata

200ml/7fl oz water

50g/2oz mature Cheddar cheese, grated

Heat the vegetable oil and sauté the onion, carrots and celery for five minutes. Rinse the lentils and add to the pan. Add the sweet potato and sauté for one minute. Pour in the passata and water. Cover and cook for about 30 minutes. Remove from the heat and stir in the cheese until melted. Purée in a blender.

Passata is simply sieved tomatoes. You can buy it in cartons and bottles in the supermarket

Lentils are a good, cheap source of protein. They also provide iron, which is important for brain development particularly between the ages of six months and two years

Let's Celebrate

Create irresistibly cute creatures to celebrate World Animal Day

Your little ones won't be able to keep their paws off them

World Animal Day 4th October

Let's Celebrate World Animal Day

Silky soft fur, boundless energy and the most loyal friend anyone could wish for. My puppy Oscar is part of the family and my children absolutely adore him. Kids and animals are a match made in heaven – they're both so full of enthusiasm, curiosity and fun.

So we'll certainly be enjoying World Animal Day on 4th October. It's a celebration of the beauty, diversity and special role of animals in our world. It's a wonderful excuse for cooking some good family food too, all with an irresistible animal-shaped twist that every child will love.

I've chosen my favourite animal-themed recipes because even the fussiest eater becomes a happy bunny when faced with an animal shape on their plate.

Inspire your child's appetite with a cat's face that's really a tasty fish pie, a crocodile that's made of cucumber and a snake that's created from tuna- and cheese-topped bagels. They all look amazing and taste delicious: for

kids, food just doesn't get any better than this.

So pack a warming homemade picnic and visit the zoo to discover all creatures great and small. Share a family breakfast, then wrap up warm and head to the park to feed the ducks and chase pigeons. Or enjoy weekend teatime treats (not you, Oscar...)

Watch fussy eaters become happy bunnies

with the whole family sat around the table together, drawing pictures, playing games and chatting about their favourite animals.

While your children tuck into these special animal-inspired dishes, you know they're getting all the energy and nutrients they need. And that's yet another delicious reason to celebrate World Animal Day...

Buzzy Bees

■ Serves 10　■ Prep time: 25 mins

60ml/4 tbsp smooth peanut butter

15ml/1 tbsp honey

2 tbsp dried skimmed milk powder

1 tbsp sesame seeds

1 Weetabix, crushed

1 tbsp cocoa powder

Flaked almonds

10 currants

Cocktail sticks

Mix together the peanut butter and honey and then blend in the remaining ingredients. Form heaped teaspoons of the mixture into oval shapes to look like bees. Dip a cocktail stick into the cocoa powder and press gently onto the bees' bodies to form stripes.

Press flaked almond wings into the sides of the bee. Cut the currants in half, roll between your finger and thumb to form tiny balls, and arrange them on the bees to look like eyes. The bees can be stored in the fridge for several days.

use a cocktail stick to create the stripes

These **nutritious**, tasty bees are **great fun** and ideal for children to make because they need **no cooking** – so they'll have the **satisfaction** of creating them from start to finish

Poodle Party Cake

■ Serves a party! ■ Prep time: 50 mins ■ Cook time: 35 mins

For the cake
285g/10oz unsalted butter,
at room temperature
285g/10oz caster sugar
5 eggs
2½ tsp vanilla extract
285g/10oz self raising flour
¼ tsp salt

For the icing
170g/6oz unsalted butter,
at room temperature
340g/12oz icing sugar, sifted
Pinch salt
1 tbsp milk
Pink food colouring

For the decoration
500g/17½oz white mini marshmallows
350g/12½oz dessicated coconut
Green food colouring
4 tbsp apricot jam
Mint imperials
Yellow chocolate sweets
Length of pink ribbon
Black liquorice laces and sweets
5 liquorice twists
Pontefract cake for the nose

You will also need
A cake board 45x55cm
2 x 11cm/4in diameter saucers, (or cut
2 x 11cm/4in diameter circles from paper)
5cm/2in round cutter
Ruler
Serrated knife
Palette knife

The **birthday cake** is always the focal point of the party and it's **so much fun** to create it with your child

1 Preheat the oven to 180C/350F/Gas Mark 4. Grease and line a 20 x 27cm (8 x 10½in) rectangular cake tin. Put four paper liners in a muffin tin. To make the cake, beat the butter and sugar until pale and fluffy.

2 Beat the eggs and vanilla, and add to the butter, then sift in the flour and salt. Beat until just combined.

3 Spoon (I use an ice cream scoop) some batter into the four paper cake cases so they are half full. Spoon the rest of the batter into the prepared cake tin and spread it out so it is level.

Even **very young children** can help you decorate it with marshmallows

4 Bake the cupcakes for 18 to 20 minutes and the cake for 30 to 35 minutes, until all have risen and are golden. To check they have cooked through, insert a cocktail stick and it should come out clean. Cool the cake and cupcakes completely.

Poodle Party Cake Template

It's a good idea to get a sheet of polystyrene from an arts and crafts shop and cut out the template for the cake from this. You can then place these onto the baked sponge and cut out the body parts using a serrated knife.

5cm / 2in circle

These shapes are actual size. Use them as a guide – you can photocopy and cut around the shapes or trace around them to get the right size

2 x 11cm / 4in diameter circles

This shape is to create the poodle's head

5½ x 4½cm / 2 x 1¾in rectangle

5 Trim the top of the cake so it is level (a bread knife is good for this). Turn the cake over and place the saucers and head template on to the cake (hold templates in place with cocktail sticks) and cut around the templates with a serrated knife. From the leftover cake, cut out a rectangle, 5½ x 4½cm (2 x 1¾in), and a circle, 5cm/2in in diameter. Remove the paper cases from the cupcakes and trim the tops level. Trim a section, 1½cm/½in deep, from one of the cupcakes, so it fits to the head.

6 Assemble the main part of the cake (the poodle's body) on a large cake board, using cocktail sticks to secure it if necessary (remove the sticks before serving the cake).

To prevent your cake board becoming covered in icing, tuck pieces of baking paper under the edges of the cake

7 To make the icing, beat the butter until pale and fluffy, then blend in the icing sugar a bit at a time. Stir in the salt and milk to give a soft, spreadable consistency. Add the food colouring, drop by drop, until you get the right pink colour.

8 Cover the poodle's body with a thick layer of icing. Pull away the baking parchment and cover the top of the head and the main parts of the body in marshmallows. Position one cupcake for the tail and two for the feet, then cover in a layer of icing (sit on baking paper).

9 Trim the small cut-out circle of cake to 2cm/1in in height. Cover in a layer of icing and position on the cake, just above the front shoulder as an ear.

10 Trim the liquorice twists to fit from the body to the feet and the tail (body to feet 8cm/3in, body to tail 11cm/4in). Insert the liquorice twists to feet, tail and body (remove the baking paper). Use the remaining liquorice to create the face and use a Pontefract cake for the nose. Cover the tail in mini marshmallows and cover half of each foot in mini marshmallows.

11 Warm the apricot jam and brush over the remaining parts of the cake board. To make the grass to cover the cake board, mix the dessicated coconut with a little of the green food colouring and a few drops of water. Strew the green coconut over the cake board and press down. Decorate with daisies made from imperial mints and yellow chocolate sweets. Finally, use the pink ribbon to create a bow for the poodle.

Use the liquorice strips and Pontefract cake to create the poodle's face

Mice in Jackets

■ Serves 4　■ Prep time: 35 mins　■ Cook time: 1 hour

For the potatoes
4 small baking potatoes
(approx 250g each)
Olive oil for brushing
20g/1oz butter
5 to 6 tbsp milk
60g/2oz grated Cheddar cheese
Salt and pepper

For the decoration
4 cherry tomatoes
Chives
2 radishes
Raisins
2 spring onions

Wash the potatoes, pat dry and prick the skins in several places. Put them on a baking tray and brush them all over with the oil. Bake in a pre-heated oven at 200C/400F/Gas Mark 6 for about one hour, or until they feel soft when pressed.

When cool enough to handle, cut off the tops of the potatoes, carefully scoop out the flesh and mash it up with the butter, milk and two-thirds of the cheese until smooth, and season to taste. Spoon the mixture back into the potato skins, sprinkle with the remaining cheese and cook under the grill for a few minutes until golden.

Fix a small cherry tomato into each of the potatoes for the noses using a cocktail stick. Add some short lengths of chives for the whiskers – you can tuck these behind the tomato. Decorate with sliced radishes for the ears, raisins for the eyes and spring onion for the tails.

It's **rewarding** all round to involve children in cooking. They will **love helping** you decorate these cute potato mice

This **snappy** little number looks amazing and makes a **fabulous** prop for **healthy** snacks

you could use ham and pineapple as well as cheese

cucumber crocodile

■ Serves 4   ■ Prep time: 30 mins

1¼ cucumbers
Mixture of cheeses (Gruyère and Cheddar for example)
1 fresh pineapple, peeled and cut into cubes
Cocktail sticks
2 cherry tomatoes
1 carrot

Cut out a triangle at one end of the cucumber to make the crocodile's mouth. Cut a long strip from the carrot using a vegetable peeler. Cut this into a strip about half an inch wide and cut along one side to form a serrated edge. Cut a groove in the mouth of the crocodile to hold the carrot strip. These are the crocodile's teeth. Use a quarter of another cucumber to cut out feet for the crocodile and attach these with cocktail sticks. Chop the cheese and pineapple into cubes. Thread cheese and pineapple cubes onto each cocktail stick and spear the sticks into the cucumber. Cut a cocktail stick in half and use these to attach the cherry tomatoes to form the crocodile's eyes.

Annabel's party tips

🐾 The most successful parties are where the children actively participate. Encourage your children to make their own invitations, help organise party games, be involved in decorating the room by blowing up balloons and help prepare some of the food.

🐾 Forward planning and organisation are the secrets to success. You can freeze some of the food, such as cookies and cakes, in advance. If you want an outdoor party, make sure there is a contingency plan for an indoor venue if it rains.

🐾 Don't make the party too long. Better that they leave wanting more!

cheesy Bread Animals

■ Serves 6　■ Prep time: 40 mins plus 45 mins for rising　■ Cook time: 20 mins

For the bread
250g/8oz strong plain flour
(plus plain flour to dust)
Pinch of salt
1 x 7g/¼oz fast-action yeast sachet
½ tsp honey
Pinch of cayenne pepper
1 tsp mustard powder
150ml/6fl oz warm water
50g/2oz grated mature Cheddar cheese
3 tbsp freshly grated Parmesan cheese

For the decoration
1 egg
Currants
Sesame seeds
Pumpkin seeds
Poppy seeds
Grated Cheddar cheese

how many different animals can you make?

Preheat the oven to 200C/400F/Gas Mark 6. Sift the flour and salt into a mixing bowl. Stir in the yeast, honey, cayenne pepper and mustard, and just enough of the water to form a soft dough. Transfer to a floured surface and knead lightly for about 10 minutes to make smooth, pliable dough. Use the heel of your hand to work the dough. Pat it into a circle, about 20cm/8in across, spread the grated cheese over it, then fold the dough in half. Fold again, so the cheese is enclosed. Knead for one to two minutes to work in the cheese – this will produce a slightly streaky effect.

Shape the dough into six animal figures (see below) and transfer to a floured baking sheet. Cover them loosely with a tea towel and leave to rise in a warm place for about 45 minutes. They are ready to bake when they are roughly double their original size.

Brush the risen dough with beaten egg and add currants for eyes. Sprinkle the tops with sesame seeds, poppy seeds, pumpkin seeds or grated cheese. Transfer to the preheated oven and bake for 20 minutes, or until golden brown. The underside should sound hollow when tapped. Leave on a wire rack to cool.

Animal magic

Divide the dough into six balls and keep in a bowl covered with a clean and damp cloth

TEDDY BEAR Use one of the divided dough and split into three balls: one will be used for a body, one will be for a head, and the third for body parts. Make seven small balls for legs, hands, ears, and a nose. Attach all the body parts into a bear shape and add currants for eyes and a belly button.

HEDGEHOG Use a pair of scissors to cut spikes on one dough ball. Use currants for eyes and nose.

TORTOISE Divide one dough ball in half – one for the body and the other for body parts. Divide one half into six and attach to the body. Add currants for eyes. Using a small knife, make marks as the pattern on the shell.

This is a **fun** way of serving **bagels** and you can make the snake as long as you like depending on how many bagels you use. It's really **quick and easy**

chocolate Teddy Bear cupcakes

■ Makes 8   ■ Prep time: 10 mins   ■ Cook time: 20 mins

For the cake:
55g/2oz plain chocolate
55g/2oz butter
65g/2¼oz dark brown sugar
1 egg, beaten
½ tsp vanilla
4 tbsp sour cream
55g/2oz plain flour
1 tbsp cocoa
½ tsp baking powder

For the buttercream:
75g/2½oz plain chocolate
75g/2½oz butter, at room temp
2 tbsp icing sugar
Pinch of salt

For decoration:
Ready-to-roll white icing
Chocolate buttons
Chocolate M&M's
Black writing icing

Preheat oven to 180C/350F/Gas Mark 4. Line a muffin tin with eight cake cases. Melt the dark chocolate over a pan of hot water then allow to cool for five minutes. Cream the butter and brown sugar until fluffy, then beat in the cooled chocolate, followed by the egg, vanilla and sour cream. Sift the flour, cocoa and baking powder, plus a large pinch of salt, into the bowl and fold in. Spoon into the cake cases (about two-thirds full). Bake for 18-20 minutes, until risen and firm to the touch. Cool on a wire rack.

To make the buttercream, melt the dark chocolate over a pan of warm water, then allow to cool for five minutes. Beat the butter and sugar together with a pinch of salt, then beat in the cooled chocolate. The icing will be very soft, so refrigerate for 20-30 minutes, stirring every 10 minutes, until firmer, but spreadable.

Swirl the buttercream over the cakes using a palette knife and refrigerate for about an hour, until icing has set.

Make eight small balls of white icing and flatten into oval shapes. Place in the centre of each cupcake and attach an M&M for the nose using a little of the writing icing. Draw on a mouth using the writing icing and add chocolate buttons for ears and M&M's for eyes. Make pupils using blobs of the black writing icing.

Bagel Snake

■ Serves 4   ■ Prep time: 25 mins
■ Cook time: 10 mins

200g/7oz can of tuna in oil, drained
2 tbsp ketchup
2 tbsp crème fraîche or Greek yoghurt
2 spring onions, finely sliced
2 to 3 hard boiled eggs (boil for 10 minutes)
3 tbsp mayonnaise
1 tbsp fresh chives, snipped
3 tbsp salad cress
Salt and freshly ground black pepper
Chives
Cherry tomatoes, halved
1 stuffed olive, sliced
A strip of sweet pepper

Slice the bagels in half and cut each piece in half again down the centre to form semi-circles. Cut out the head of the snake from one of the pieces of bagel and the tail from another. Mix the ingredients for the tuna salad topping and for the egg salad topping. Spread half of the bagels with tuna and half with egg.

Decorate the bagels with the tuna topping with halved cherry tomatoes, then decorate those with the egg topping with strips of chives, arranged in a criss-cross pattern. Arrange the bagels to form the body of a snake. Attach the head to the snake's body and arrange two slices of stuffed olive to form the eyes. Cut out a forked tongue from the strip of sweet pepper.

These delicious cupcakes are so easy to make and your child will have such fun decorating each one – not to mention stirring the cake mix. They really are a chocolatey treat for the whole family

Oil-rich fish such as salmon and sardines are especially good brain boosters because of their omega-3 essential fats – vital for brain function

This delicious fish pie is a great first step to liking fish. So help your little kitten be a healthy fish-eater. The cat's face makes it even more fun to eat

Annabel's Mini Fish Pie

■ Serves 3   ■ Prep time: 35 mins   ■ Cook time: 30 mins
■ Suitable for freezing

For the pie
375g/13oz potatoes, peeled and diced
1½ tbsp milk
55g/2oz butter
A little salt and pepper (for age 1+)
25g/1oz onion, peeled and finely chopped
1 tbsp flour
75ml/3fl oz milk
50ml/2fl oz vegetable stock
125g/4½oz cod fillet, skinned and cubed
125g/4½oz salmon fillet, skinned and cubed
1 tsp chopped fresh parsley

1 bay leaf
25g/1oz frozen peas
50g/2oz Cheddar cheese, grated
1 egg, lightly beaten

For the decoration
Cherry tomatoes
Cooked green beans
Red pepper
Basil leaves
Chives and rosemary

Preheat the oven to 180C/350F/Gas Mark 4. Bring a pan of lightly salted water to the boil, add the potatoes, reduce the heat and cook for 15 to 20 minutes, or until tender. Drain the potatoes and mash together with the milk and half of the butter until smooth, and then season to taste for babies and children over one.

Melt the remaining butter in a saucepan, add the onion and sauté until softened. Add the flour and cook for 30 seconds, stirring. Gradually stir in the milk and then the stock. Bring to the boil and cook for one minute. Add the fish with the parsley and bay leaf. Simmer for about three minutes and then stir in the peas and cook for one minute. Remove the bay leaf and stir in the cheese until melted. Season with a little salt and pepper.

Divide the fish between three ramekin dishes and top each one with the mashed potato mixture. Brush this with the lightly beaten egg. Bake in the oven for 15 minutes and finish them off under a preheated grill until golden.

To create the cat's face, use slices of cherry tomatoes and chives for the eyes, green beans for the mouth, red pepper cut into a triangle for the nose, basil leaves for the ears and rosemary for the whiskers.

Growing personality growing appetite

Feed your **toddler's curiosity** with intriguing and **tasty meals**. Help them **enjoy** their thrilling new independence by **encouraging** them to feed themselves

Growing personality, growing appetite

As soon as your young child learns to walk, they'll love exploring the fascinating world around them. A simple winter walk becomes an incredible adventure; splashing in puddles, learning new words, picking up sticks and practising new skills such as going up and down a step over and over (and over) again… It all helps your busy toddler begin to understand their amazing world.

Now you can set off on a voyage of delicious food discovery together. Inspire your child's curiosity by offering them new ways to eat, such as my Crispy Sweet Chilli Chicken Fingers (p55) to pick, dip and lick. Tempt your toddler with healthy homemade versions of children's favourites such as Funny Face Beefburgers (p56) flavoured with grated apple, balsamic vinegar, thyme and oyster sauce – so tasty the whole family will want to tuck in.

Their growing appetite means now your little one can enjoy little versions of proper family meals. They'll feel very grown-up with their own individual Vegetarian

Shepherd's Pie (p63), all to themselves.

Encouraging your toddler to feed themselves, and warmly praising their efforts, is a wonderful confidence boost for them. Learning to handle their own spoon or fork also helps little hands tackle dressing, drawing and writing later on.

Now your little one can enjoy proper meals

As their unique and powerful personality develops, your toddler will love expressing their opinions in no uncertain terms. This growing independence gives you a chance to offer your child new flavours and textures – and some might say an opportunity to develop more patience! One thing's for sure, there won't be a problem with getting feedback as your little one revels in their new communication skills…

chinese-Style Rice With chicken and Prawns

■ Serves 6　■ Prep time: 15 mins plus 10 mins for marinating　■ Cook time: 25 mins

For the rice

1 chicken breast (about 150g
cut into small cubes)

60g/2oz carrot, peeled and diced

4 tbsp vegetable oil

1 small onion, peeled and finely chopped

Salt and white pepper

1 beaten egg

60g/2oz frozen peas

1 large spring onion, sliced

60g/2oz tinned sweetcorn

125g/4½oz small cooked prawns

175g/6oz basmati rice, rinsed in cold
water and then drained

For the marinade

1 tbsp soy sauce

1 tbsp sake

½ tsp sesame oil

1 tbsp caster sugar

Mix together the ingredients for the marinade and marinate the chicken for 10 minutes.

Meanwhile, cook the rice in boiling, lightly salted water according to the instructions on the packet. Steam the diced carrot for eight minutes and, halfway through, add the peas so that they are steamed for four minutes.

Heat the oil in a wok or large frying pan, add the onion and sauté for three minutes. Season the beaten egg with a little salt and white pepper, pour it into a small frying pan, tipping the pan to spread it evenly, and cook until set. Remove from the heat, slide out the omelette, roll up and cut into fine slices.

Drain the marinade from the chicken and reserve. Add the chicken to the onion in the wok and sauté for three to four minutes until cooked. Add the spring onion, carrots, peas and sweetcorn and cook for one minute.

Add the cooked rice and prawns, and toss the rice over a high heat for two minutes. Add the strips of egg and the reserved marinade from the chicken and heat through.

Egg fried rice with chicken, prawns and fresh veg makes a complete meal, and is popular with children of all ages

crispy sweet-chilli chicken Fingers

■ Serves 4   ■ Prep time: 20 mins   ■ Cook time: 15 mins   ■ Suitable for freezing before cooking

For the chicken

2 chicken breasts (250g/8oz), cut into eight strips each

150g/6oz bag sweet chilli crisps

25g/5 tbsp grated Parmesan

4 tbsp flour

1 large egg

Freshly ground pepper

For the marinade

200ml/7fl oz buttermilk

1 tsp Worcestershire sauce

1 tsp soy sauce

1 small clove garlic, crushed

½ tsp paprika

½ tsp dried oregano

For the sauce

2 tbsp tomato ketchup/sauce

½ tsp sweet chilli sauce

2 tsp lime juice

Add a bit more sweet chilli sauce if your children like hot foods

To make the nuggets, put the ingredients for the marinade in a large bowl and stir together until well mixed. Coat the chicken in the marinade and leave for at least one hour. Put the crisps into a large plastic bag and scrunch with your fingers until they become small crumbs. Pour the crumbs onto a large plate and mix in the Parmesan.

Put the flour in a bowl and mix in a little pepper. Beat the egg in a bowl with a tablespoon of cold water. Dip the chicken in the flour, egg and then the crumbs.

Arrange the chicken on a baking sheet (no need to grease) and bake in the oven for 15 minutes (turn the chicken over halfway through cooking).

To make the dipping sauce, simply mix together the ketchup, sweet chilli sauce and lime juice in a small bowl. Allow the chicken to cool slightly before eating and serve with the dipping sauce or ketchup.

These **tasty chicken fingers** are **perfect** for your toddler. They'll **love dipping them** in the sauce themselves

chicken and corn chowder

■ Makes 4   ■ Prep time: 12 mins
■ Cook time: 20 mins   ■ Suitable for freezing

1 tbsp butter

1 large shallot, finely chopped

1 medium potato (200g/7oz), peeled and diced into 1cm cubes

400g/14oz can sweetcorn, drained

650ml/22fl oz good chicken stock

6 tbsp double cream

50g/2oz shredded, cooked chicken

1 tbsp chopped parsley (optional), to serve

Melt the butter in a large saucepan and sauté the shallot for five minutes, until soft. Add the potato, corn and stock, bring to a simmer and cook until the potato is soft. Blend half of this mixture until smooth, then return to the pan and stir in the double cream. Season to taste. Stir in the shredded chicken. Serve with a little chopped parsley scattered on top if you wish.

use spaghetti
for straight hair
or macaroni
for curls

56

Funny Face Beefburgers

■ Makes 4 ■ Prep time: 20 mins ■ Cook time: 20 mins ■ Suitable for freezing

For the burgers

1 tbsp olive oil

1 large shallot, finely chopped

¼ apple, peeled, cored and grated

½ small clove garlic, crushed

1 tsp balsamic vinegar

¼ tsp thyme or finely chopped parsley

2 tsp honey

150g/6oz lean minced beef

2 tbsp grated Parmesan

1 tbsp tomato ketchup

1 tbsp oyster sauce

1 slice bread, crust removed, crumbed

sunflower oil, for frying

For the decoration

1 thin slice cheese

8 cooked peas

Halved cherry tomatoes

Strips of tomato or red pepper

120g/4oz spaghetti or macaroni

Basil leaves

4 tbsp tomato ketchup or tomato sauce

Sauté the shallot in the oil for two to three minutes, until soft. Add the apple and garlic, and cook for two to three minutes, until the apple is soft. Add the balsamic vinegar and cook for one to two minutes, until evaporated. Stir in the thyme and honey. Transfer to a bowl and allow to cool slightly. Add the remaining ingredients and mix together. Form into four burgers. Chill for one or two hours, or until needed.

Cook the pasta according to the packet instructions. Drain and toss with the tomato ketchup or sauce. Heat a large, non-stick frying pan and grease with a small amount of oil. Fry the burgers over a medium heat for about four minutes per side, until cooked through. Alternatively, you can grill them for four to five minutes per side.

Arrange some pasta on a plate as hair and sit the burgers under the hair. Add eyes made from peas, a nose from a small triangle of cheese and a mouth from tomato or pepper. Serve any leftover pasta in a separate bowl.

The burgers can be covered and refrigerated until needed. They can also be frozen for up to one month – wrap each burger individually in clingfilm and freeze on a tray. When solid, transfer to a bag or box. The burgers can be removed individually and defrosted overnight in the fridge or for one to two hours at room temperature. Cook and serve as above.

These are great for kids provided they are made with quality lean minced beef. Use any lean steak and whizz it in a food processor

If you prefer less topping, this makes enough for three split muffins or six mini pizzas

This takes just a few minutes to create and makes a delicious snack at any time of the day

Toasted Tuna Muffin

■ Makes 2　■ Prep time: 10 mins　■ Cook time: 2 mins

200g/7oz tin tuna

2 tbsp tomato ketchup

1 tbsp Greek yoghurt

1 tbsp mayonnaise

1 large spring onion, finely chopped

2 breakfast muffins, split in half

40g (1½oz) grated Cheddar cheese

Preheat the grill to high. Drain and flake the tuna into a bowl and mix with the tomato ketchup, Greek yoghurt, mayonnaise and spring onion.

Split the muffins and lightly toast them. Pile the tuna mix onto the cut sides and cover with the grated cheese. Grill for one or two minutes until golden and bubbling. Cool slightly before serving.

These **fishcakes** are **crumbed**, so they aren't too squishy to survive **being picked up**, but for older children, who eat with a fork, you could just dust them in flour before frying. The **ketchup** in this recipe gives a subtle tang – add more if you like

These salmon balls are suitable for freezing and they can be cooked straight from frozen

Tasty Salmon Balls

■ Makes 14　■ Prep time: 20 mins　■ Cook time: 30 mins　■ Suitable for freezing

500ml/18fl oz fish or vegetable stock
150g/6oz salmon fillet (skin on)
1 medium potato
2 small spring onions, finely chopped
1 tbsp mayonnaise
4 tsp tomato ketchup
2 tbsp plain flour
1 egg, beaten
3 tbsp dried breadcrumbs
2 tbsp grated Parmesan
5 to 6 tbsp oil, for frying

Put the stock in a medium-sized saucepan and bring to a simmer. Add the salmon, flesh side down, and cook at a very gentle simmer for seven minutes. Turn the salmon over and cook for a further two to three minutes until the fish is opaque and breaks into large flakes when pressed with a fork. Transfer to a plate and allow to cool slightly before peeling off the skin.

Microwave the potato for seven to nine minutes (depending on wattage) until soft. Leave to stand for 10 minutes, or until cool enough to handle, and then peel off the skin with a sharp knife. Alternatively, boil the whole potato, with the skin on, for about 30 minutes in a pan of salted water, allow to cool and then peel off the skin.

Put the potato in a bowl and mash well. Flake the salmon and stir it into the potato, along with the onion, mayonnaise and ketchup. Season to taste. Mix well – you don't want any large pieces of salmon. Roll tablespoons of the mixture into balls.

Put the flour on a plate, put the egg in a bowl and mix the breadcrumbs and Parmesan together on a separate plate. Dust the balls with flour, then dip in the egg and coat in breadcrumbs. For best results, cover and refrigerate overnight.

Heat the oil in a frying pan and cook the fishcakes for about one minute on each side, until golden. Drain on kitchen paper and allow to cool before serving.

Pasta is a good source of complex carbohydrates, boosting your child's energy levels and providing a good source of protein and calcium

Baked Macaroni cheese with Ham and Tomato

■ Serves 6 ■ Prep time: 15 mins ■ Cook time: 15 mins
■ Suitable for freezing

For the macaroni
45g/1½oz butter
45g/1½oz flour
450ml/15fl oz milk
85g/3oz Gruyère cheese, grated
60g/2oz Parmesan cheese, grated
150g/5oz mascarpone
350g/12oz macaroni
4 medium tomatoes, skinned, deseeded
and chopped
75g/3oz sliced ham, shredded (optional)

For the topping
40g/1½oz breadcrumbs (2 slices white
or wholemeal bread, crusts removed)
20g/1oz Parmesan cheese, grated

Cook the pasta in plenty of salted boiling water according to the packet instructions.
Melt the butter, stir in the flour and cook for one minute. Gradually add the milk, stirring
over a low heat for five to six minutes. Take off the heat, stir in the Gruyère and Parmesan
until melted, and then stir in the mascarpone.

Drain the pasta and return to the pan, and pour over the cheese sauce. Heat through
gently. Stir in the chopped tomatoes and shredded ham.

Transfer to a greased ovenproof dish, 26 x 17 x 5cm (10 x 6.5 x 2in). Mix together the
breadcrumbs and Parmesan, and sprinkle on top. Place under a preheated grill, set to high,
until golden and bubbling.

you can make this with broccoli instead of ham and tomato

Pies can be wrapped in clingfilm and frozen. Defrost overnight in the fridge

Lentils are a good source of protein and iron for vegetarians, and green lentils make a savoury and satisfying base for this shepherd's pie

Vegetarian Shepherd's Pie

- 4 to 6 portions (4 mini baking dishes or 6 ramekins)
- Prep time: 15 mins
- Cook time: 30 mins
- Suitable for freezing

For the filling

1 tbsp olive oil

1 medium red onion, finely chopped

1 medium carrot, peeled and grated

1 clove garlic, crushed

150g/5oz green lentils, rinsed

400g tin chopped tomatoes

350ml/12fl oz vegetable stock

150ml/6fl oz water

2 tbsp tomato purée

1 tbsp soy sauce

4 tsp brown sugar

5 tbsp frozen peas (optional)

For the topping

750g/1.7lbs potatoes, peeled and cubed

20g/1oz butter

4 tbsp milk

1 egg, lightly beaten

50g/2oz grated Cheddar cheese (optional)

Salt and freshly ground black pepper

Preheat the oven to 200C/400F/Gas Mark 6. Heat the oil in a large saucepan and sauté the onion and carrot for eight to 10 minutes, stirring occasionally, until soft and starting to brown. Add the garlic and cook for one minute, then stir in the lentils, tomatoes, stock, water, tomato purée, soy sauce and sugar. Bring to the boil, reduce the heat and simmer for 40 to 45 minutes, until the lentils are soft (older lentils will take a little longer). Add a little extra water if the pan gets too dry.

Meanwhile, boil the potatoes in plenty of salted water for about 15 minutes, until just tender. Drain the potatoes and mash well. Beat in the butter and milk and season to taste with salt and pepper.

Season the lentils to taste with pepper then divide them between small baking dishes or ramekins. I used six ramekin dishes (9cm diameter, 4cm depth). Spread the mashed potato over the lentils and mark in ridges with a fork. Refrigerate until needed.

Put the pies on a baking sheet, brush the tops with the beaten egg or sprinkle with grated cheese and bake for 25 to 30 minutes, until the potato is golden on top and the pie is piping hot. Cool slightly and check temperature before serving.

Yummy winter lunches

Kids bored of sandwiches? Try these **refreshingly tasty** and **healthy** ideas that will help keep your child excited by what's in their **lunchbox** – so they bring it home empty!

Tasty lunchbox ideas

Children are all different, but, by and large, what they want is a quick fix – try some of these suggestions for a great packed lunch.

Most children will leave food that takes a lot of effort to eat because they want a quick refuelling stop so they can carry on playing with their friends. Try giving your children some prepared fruit, such as a peeled clementine (protected with clingfilm) or a halved kiwi fruit so they can scoop out the flesh with a teaspoon.

Lunches can be prepared the night before to save time the next morning. You can include pasta salads, sandwich fillings, fruit compotes – or pick something from last night's dinner, such as soup in a flask.

Add a personal touch to your child's lunch by tucking in a note, stickers or a joke, or send a special treat labelled 'for my best friend' – there are lots of delicious cookies you can make with your child in this book. Pack fun napkins, decorate lunch bags with stickers or draw a face on a banana with a marker pen.

If your child likes to trade or share at lunchtime, include an extra delicious treat, such as Rice Krispie squares, chocolate muffins or popcorn – label it 'For a Friend' if you like.

Always keep a supply of frozen bread, rolls, bagels or pitta bread in the freezer for emergencies.

However healthy food is, it won't get eaten unless it's tasty and appealing to your child. Simple touches can make all the difference. Cut sandwiches into shapes using cookie cutters or thread fruit onto a straw to make a fresh fruit skewer.

According to the recent Foods Standards Agency survey, nine out of 10 lunchboxes contain double the recommended daily intake of sugar and nearly half the daily allowance of salt and saturated fats. Try to avoid too many processed foods because these are the ones that tend to contain fewer nutrients and too much salt, sugar and fat.

Salads make a nice change from sandwiches. Try Chicken Caesar salad or a chicken and potato salad using a shop-bought potato salad and mixing in chicken, tomatoes and spring onion.

Give them pure fruit juice or water – some juice drinks contain very little juice, but a lot of sugar, so look at the label before buying. Pure fruit juices contain 100% juice, but a fruit juice drink can contain as little as 5% juice and as much as five teaspoons of sugar in one carton.

Sandwiches don't need to be boring – there are so many different types of bread available. Try sushi-style rolls stuffed with tuna, carrot and cucumber, tortilla wraps with cooked chicken, lettuce and tomato, or bagels with ham and cheese, or cream cheese and smoked salmon. To prevent sandwiches becoming squashed, store them in a small plastic container in your child's lunchbox.

It's important to include fresh fruit in your child's lunchbox – you can cut up wedges of mango, melon, papaya and pineapple, and pack them in a plastic container. Alternatively, make fruit skewers from a selection of fresh fruit.

As the colder weather sets in, it's a good idea to include something hot in a lunchbox. A wide-mouthed mini Thermos flask would be ideal for serving up a delicious cup of home-made or shop-bought soup, which is both warming and nutritious. You can put baked beans or pasta shapes with tomato sauce in a flask.

Children like raw vegetables such as carrot sticks, sweet pepper and cucumber. Wrap these in damp kitchen paper to prevent them from drying out and maybe include a tasty dip, such as cream cheese with chives or houmous.

Sandwich fillings

Get rid of boring sandwiches forever with this selection of yummy fillings

Despite sandwiches being a great British institution, children – like adults – can become tired of the same old triangles. Supermarkets have helped enormously in recent years by supplying bread from around the globe, including pitta pockets, bagels, ciabatta and baguettes.
To keep sandwiches fresh, wrap them in plastic wrap or foil and buy a small plastic box to put them in – this also stops them getting squashed.

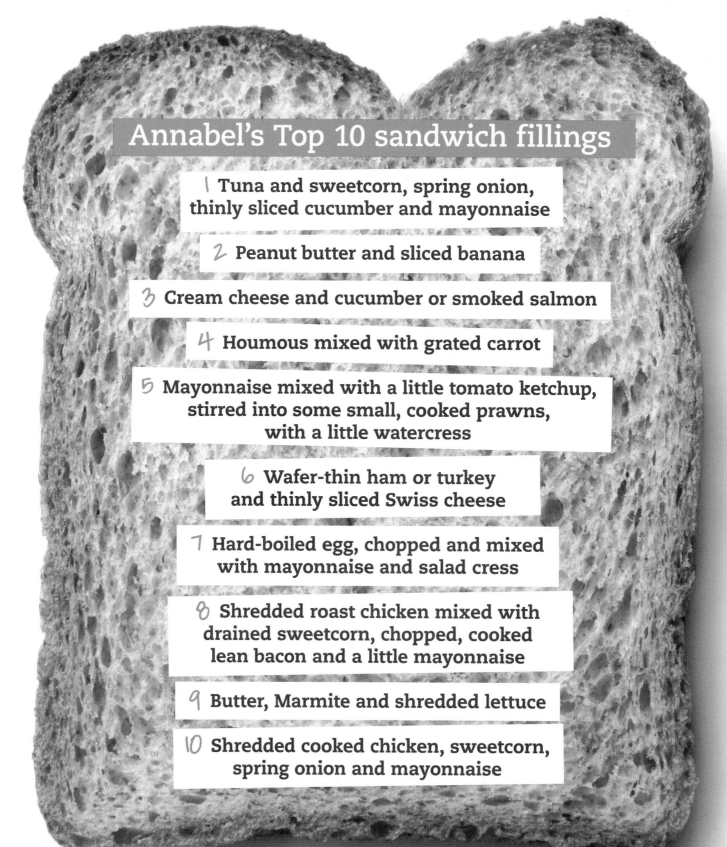

Annabel's Top 10 sandwich fillings

1 Tuna and sweetcorn, spring onion, thinly sliced cucumber and mayonnaise

2 Peanut butter and sliced banana

3 Cream cheese and cucumber or smoked salmon

4 Houmous mixed with grated carrot

5 Mayonnaise mixed with a little tomato ketchup, stirred into some small, cooked prawns, with a little watercress

6 Wafer-thin ham or turkey and thinly sliced Swiss cheese

7 Hard-boiled egg, chopped and mixed with mayonnaise and salad cress

8 Shredded roast chicken mixed with drained sweetcorn, chopped, cooked lean bacon and a little mayonnaise

9 Butter, Marmite and shredded lettuce

10 Shredded cooked chicken, sweetcorn, spring onion and mayonnaise

Sushi-style rolls **stuffed** with a **nutritious** filling are great for **lunchboxes** – prepare the **filling** the night before to **save time**

Try these eggs-periments!

Q. How do you know your eggs are fresh?

A. Place the egg in a glass or small bowl of water. If it stays at the bottom, it's very fresh. If it tilts up slightly, it's up to a week old. If it floats, throw it away.

Q. How can you tell if an egg is hard boiled?

A. Spin the egg on a flat surface. Place your finger on top of the egg to stop it moving and then take it away immediately. If the egg is raw, it continues to spin.

Kiddie Sushi-Style Roll

■ Serves 1 ■ Prep time: 5 mins

2 slices white bread, crusts removed
100g can tuna in oil, drained
2 tbsp mayonnaise
1½ tbsp ketchup
2 drops Tabasco sauce (or to taste)
5cm piece of cucumber, cut into strips
5cm piece of carrot, peeled and coarsely grated

Use a rolling pin to flatten the bread to a quarter-inch thick. Mix the tuna with half of the mayonnaise, the ketchup and the Tabasco. Spread the remaining mayonnaise on the bread and spoon the tuna in a line, half an inch from one edge of each slice. Arrange cucumber on one side of the tuna and carrot on the other. Roll up from the filled end and press down to seal. Trim the ends using a sharp knife, then cut into three. You can prepare this the night before, wrap the rolls in clingfilm, then unwrap and cut each into three pieces in the morning.

Other fillings: Canned salmon mixed with mayonnaise, ketchup and spring onion, with cucumber strips; Strips of Cheddar with slices of tomato and cucumber; Houmous with grated carrot, shredded lettuce and chopped tomato.

Lara's chicken wraps

■ Serves 4 ■ Prep time: 10 mins plus 20 minutes to marinate

Marinate and cook the chicken the night before or buy ready-cooked marinated chicken.

For the filling

2 skinned chicken breasts
1 tbsp sunflower oil
4 large flour tortillas
4 tomatoes, cut into strips
A handful of iceberg lettuce, shredded
4 tbsp mayonnaise
Salt and freshly ground black pepper

For the marinade

1 tbsp olive oil
1 tbsp fresh lemon juice
1 garlic clove, lightly crushed
1 tbsp dark soy sauce
1 tbsp clear honey
½ tbsp brown sugar
2 tbsp sunflower oil

Score the chicken with a sharp knife. Mix together all the ingredients for the marinade and marinate the chicken for about 20 minutes.

Brush a griddle pan with oil. Remove the chicken from the marinade and, when the griddle is hot, griddle the chicken for about four minutes on each side or until cooked through. Cut into strips and set aside.

Spread each tortilla with one tablespoon of mayonnaise and arrange the chicken strips in a line, down one side of the tortilla, about 4cm/1½in from the edge the tortilla. Place a line of shredded lettuce down one side of the chicken and tomato strips down the other, and season. Roll up, cut each tortilla in half and wrap in foil to serve.

> **Wraps** are a great alternative to sandwiches and this is a **favourite** with my daughter, Lara. Like many children, she becomes fixated with one recipe and would like to **eat it every day**

Prawn and avocado wrap

■ Serves 1 to 2
■ Prep time: 10 mins

¼ avocado, chopped
1 tsp lemon juice
½ medium tomato, deseeded and diced
1 spring onion, sliced
30g/1oz small cooked prawns
1 tbsp mayonnaise
½ tsp tomato ketchup
Salt and freshly ground black pepper
1 small flour tortilla

Put the avocado and lemon juice in a small bowl, and toss together until the avocado is coated with the juice. Add the tomato, spring onion, prawns, mayonnaise and ketchup, and combine. Season with salt and pepper. Spoon onto one half of a tortilla and roll up. Cut in half and wrap in foil. Advise your child to unwrap the tortilla slowly as he/she eats it to keep the filling contained.

Turkey wrap with plum sauce

■ Serves 4 ■ Prep time: 10 mins ■ Cook time: 5 mins

225g/8oz cooked, shredded turkey meat
A little plum sauce
A few drops sesame oil
4 tbsp mayonnaise
1½ tsp soy sauce

Half small cucumber, peeled and cut into matchsticks
2 large spring onions, finely sliced
1½ tsp toasted sesame seeds (optional)
4 small flour tortillas

Arrange the turkey on a baking sheet. Spread a little plum sauce on top, sprinkle with sesame oil and grill for about five minutes, until browned. For a no-cook variation, mix the turkey meat with a little plum sauce and leave out the sesame oil.

Mix together the mayonnaise and soy sauce. Stir in the turkey, cucumber and spring onion, and sprinkle the sesame seeds (if using) on top.

Heat the tortilla for a few seconds in a microwave or in a dry frying pan – or, if putting in a lunchbox, use the tortilla straight from the packet. Arrange the filling down one side of each tortilla and roll up. Cut in half, diagonally, and wrap in foil.

This home-made tomato soup is particularly delicious. It's great nice and hot, poured into a Thermos flask in your child's lunchbox on a cold day

Homemade Tomato Soup

■ Serves 4 ■ Prep time: 15 mins ■ Cook time: 45 mins ■ Suitable for freezing

2 tbsp light olive oil

1 onion, peeled and chopped

1 garlic clove, crushed

200g/7oz carrots, peeled and diced

500g/1lb ripe plum tomatoes, skinned and roughly chopped

200ml/7fl oz passata

400ml/14fl oz vegetable or chicken stock

1 bay leaf

Large sprig of fresh thyme

100ml/4fl oz single cream (optional)

Salt and freshly ground black pepper

Small handful of basil leaves (optional)

Cover the tomatoes with boiling water and leave for one minute. Remove with a slotted spoon and plunge into cold water, and the skins should then peel away easily. Roughly chop the tomatoes and remove the seeds.

Heat the oil in a large saucepan. Sauté the onion, garlic and carrots for six to seven minutes. Stir in the tomatoes, passata, stock, bay leaf and thyme, and bring to a simmer. Cover and cook for 35 to 40 minutes. Remove the bay leaf and the stalk from the thyme (most of the thyme leaves will have dropped off by now). Blend in a food processor until smooth, stir in the cream (if using) and season with salt and pepper. Add some torn basil leaves if you like.

My children love **minestrone** and this is a favourite recipe. **Haricot beans** are rich in protein, vitamins and minerals

Minestrone is a classic **Italian** soup that can be made **all year round** using whatever vegetables are **in season**

Mummy's Minestrone Soup

■ Serves 8 ■ Prep time: 15 mins ■ Cook time: 45 mins
■ Suitable for freezing

2 tbsp olive oil
1 carrot, peeled and finely diced
1 stick celery, finely diced
1 small red onion, finely diced
1 clove garlic, crushed
5 ripe plum tomatoes, peeled, seeded and roughly chopped
1 tbsp tomato purée

4 pints vegetable or chicken stock
100g/4oz green cabbage, finely sliced
8 leaves fresh basil, torn into pieces
50g/2oz small pasta shapes
415g/14oz tin baked beans
Salt and freshly ground black pepper
Grated Parmesan cheese to serve (if serving at home)

Heat the olive oil in a large saucepan. Add the carrot, celery, onion and garlic, and sauté for 10 minutes, stirring occasionally. Add the tomatoes, tomato purée and stock, bring to the simmer and cook for 15 minutes. Stir in the cabbage, basil, pasta and beans, and simmer for 15 to 18 minutes until the cabbage and pasta are tender. Season with salt and pepper.

Bagels suitable for freezing on their own, but not when filled

Whether you opt for a filling of **fish, cheese** or **meat**, a nutritious **bagel** makes a tasty change to your child's **lunchbox**

Bagels

■ Serves 1　■ Prep time: 3 mins　■ Suitable from 2 years

Smoked Salmon and Cream Cheese

1½ tbsp cream cheese
½ tsp snipped chives
1 bagel
A few slices of cucumber (optional)
50g/2oz (2 slices) smoked salmon
Squeeze of lemon juice
Freshly ground black pepper (optional)

Mix together the cheese and chives, and spread over the bagel. Lay the salmon and cucumber (if using) on top, and finish with a little lemon juice and pepper (if using).

Ham and Cheese

1 bagel
Soft margarine or softened butter
Lettuce leaf
1 large thin slice Swiss cheese
1 slice turkey or ham
4 thin slices cucumber
1 tbsp mayonnaise

Butter the bagel, arrange the lettuce leaf, cheese, ham and cucumber on top. Add a blob of mayonnaise.

Tomato, Mozzarella and Basil

1 bagel
Soft margarine or butter
A few slices of mozzarella
1 tomato, sliced
2 tsp fresh pesto
A few basil leaves

Butter the bagel. Arrange the mozzarella and sliced tomato on top. Season with a little salt. Add the pesto and some basil leaves.

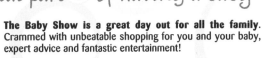

Bagels are versatile, being great with sweet and savoury fillings

Annabel's Apricot cookies

■ Makes 18　■ Prep time: 7 mins
■ Cook time: 15 mins　■ Suitable for freezing

These are also good served cold straight from the fridge

100g/4oz unsalted butter
100g/4oz cream cheese
100g/4oz caster sugar
75g/3oz plain flour
50g/2oz chopped dried apricots
65g/2oz white chocolate chips or chopped white chocolate

Preheat the oven to 180C/350F/Gas Mark 4. In a large mixing bowl, cream together the butter and cream cheese. Add the sugar and beat until fluffy. Gradually add the flour and then fold in the apricots and chocolate. The dough will be quite soft, but don't worry.

Drop heaped teaspoons of the mixture onto non-stick or lined baking sheets and bake in the oven for about 15 minutes or until lightly golden. Allow them to cook and harden for a few minutes before removing them from the baking sheet and transferring them to a wire rack.

These are a rather unusual, but totally irresistible, combination of dried apricots, cream cheese and white chocolate. They take just a few minutes to prepare and you will find them easy to make, even if you have never made cookies before

Kids  Cooking

Enjoy cooking together, step by step, spending quality time with your child – and sharing delicious results!

Kids ♡ Cooking

When it's wet and wintry outside, staying cosy indoors and cooking delicious homemade food together is a wonderful way to spend your day. I've selected some easy, yet tasty, recipes that you and your child will love making together.

Like many families, we always seem so busy and are constantly dashing about. I find cooking at home with my children creates real quality time. It's a rare chance to relax and chat while we work at our own pace, creating good food together.

Cooking is great for boosting your child's confidence and inspiring creativity. Your child can use their imagination to produce a unique finished result they'll feel so proud of – and really enjoy eating! Try my Fluffy Marshmallow Sheep (p82), cute Puppy Dog Cupcakes (p83), yummy Peanut-Butter Bears (p89) or homemade shortbread (p90) in whatever crazy shapes your child chooses.

But cooking together is about much more than results. Weighing, measuring, pouring, cracking, mixing, kneading and tasting (all with lovely clean hands of course) enable your

child to get in touch with food. That's why I've explained each recipe step by step, so your child can understand how ingredients work together to create delicious results. You never know, you might ignite a passion for cookery that goes way beyond licking the spoon: from child cook to Michelin-starred chef maybe!

Cooking at home creates quality time

Little ones love cooking just like mummy, while bigger children enjoy the responsibility of important jobs like measuring out – and every child finds food all the more irresistible when they've made it themselves. Even the fussiest eaters will find it hard to refuse my sweetcorn fritters (p84) and gorgeous fruity apple smiles (p88) when they've made them from scratch. So pop your pinnies on, roll up those sleeves and get stuck in…

Easy cupcakes

■ Serves 10　■ Prep time: 10 mins
■ Cook time: 20 mins　■ Suitable for freezing

100g/4oz soft margarine
100g/4oz caster sugar
100g/4oz self raising flour
2 medium eggs
1 tbsp vanilla essence

Preheat oven to 180C/350F/Gas Mark 4. Put all of the ingredients into a bowl or food processor and beat together until smooth. Line a bun tin with paper cases and half fill each case with the mixture. Bake in the oven for 18 to 20 minutes until well risen and the cakes spring back when you press them with your fingertips.

These **cupcakes** are **easy to make** and your child will love creating the **cute** animals

Marshmallow Sheep cupcakes

■ Serves 5　■ Prep time: 15 mins

Large white marshmallows	100g/4oz butter, softened
Mini white marshmallows	225g/8oz icing sugar, sieved
Tube of black writing icing	1 tbsp water

To make the buttercream, sieve the icing sugar. Beat the butter in an electric mixer until creamy, then gradually stir in the icing sugar. Finally, beat in the tablespoon of water. Spread a layer of buttercream over the cupcakes using a palette knife and make a small mound of buttercream in the centre. Arrange the mini marshmallows in two circles around the edge of the cakes.

Arrange some halved mini marshmallows on top of the mound of buttercream and behind the sheep's head to prop it up. Cut the large marshmallows in half and place on either side of the sheep's face to make the ears – they will stick naturally because the cut side of the marshmallow is very sticky. Arrange some halved mini marshmallows on top of and behind the sheep's head. Draw eyes and a nose on the face using the black writing icing.

oink oink!

Pink Piggy cupcakes

■ Serves 5   ■ Prep time: 10 mins

Pink food colouring
Pink marshmallows
Black and red writing icing

See marshmallow sheep for buttercream icing. Mix a few drops of the food colouring with the buttercream and spread the pink icing on top of the cakes. Stick on a nose made from a large marshmallow and ears made from slices of marshmallow. Draw eyes and a smile using the red writing icing and make the snout using black writing icing.

Make little bones from marzipan

Puppy Dog cupcakes

■ Serves 5   ■ Prep time: 10 mins

M&M's or Smarties
Giant chocolate buttons
Black writing icing
Langue du Chat biscuits

Spread on the buttercream icing as with the marshmallow sheep, then stick on the biscuit ears and use sweets for the eyes and noses. Use black writing icing to draw on the pupils of the eyes and the mouths.

Sweetcorn Fritters

- Makes 8-10
- Prep time: 15 mins
- Cook time: 5 mins

30g/1oz flour
1 tsp baking powder
Pinch of salt
1 egg
1 tbsp maple syrup
2 tbsp milk
198g tin sweetcorn, drained
2 spring onions, finely chopped
1 to 2 tbsp sunflower oil, for frying

1   Sieve the flour, baking powder and pinch of salt into a large mixing bowl.

2   Separate the egg by tipping the yolk from one half of the shell to the other. Let the egg white fall into one bowl; drop the yolk into another.

3   Add the maple syrup and milk to the egg yolk, and whisk together. Pour this mixture over the flour. Stir everything together to make a batter.

4   Whisk the egg white until it forms stiff peaks. Be careful not to over-whisk or it will go flat.

5   Use a spatula to fold the egg white into the flour mixture, making sure to carefully stir around the side of the bowl and across the middle.

6   Tip the tinned sweetcorn and chopped spring onions into the batter mixture. Fold them in (be as light as you can).

7   Heat the oil, drop in tablespoons of the batter and cook for one to two minutes until the undersides are golden and small bubbles can be seen on the surface. Flip over and cook the other sides. Transfer to a plate lined with kitchen paper while you cook more fritters with the remaining batter, then serve.

Try these for breakfast with slices of crisply cooked bacon or bananas with extra maple syrup

Corn fritters are known in southern American states as hush puppies and the local population likes to serve them up with fried chicken

Three tablespoons of sweetcorn counts as one serving of fruit and vegetables

Multi-coloured Meringues

- Makes 30 meringues ■ Prep time: 35 mins
- Cook time: 35 mins plus 45 mins standing in oven

3 medium egg whites
Pinch of salt
150g/5oz caster or superfine sugar
½ tsp cornflour
½ tsp lemon juice
Different food colouring of your choice (pink, purple, green)

1   Preheat the oven to 130C/250F/Gas Mark 1. Line two baking sheets with baking paper. Put the egg whites and pinch of salt in a bowl and whisk to stiff peaks that don't bend over when you remove the whisk. Be careful not to overbeat – the egg whites will start to look lumpy, a bit like cotton wool, if you do this.

2   Add one tablespoon of sugar to the egg whites, whisk in, then add a second and whisk back to stiff peaks. Whisk in the rest of the sugar. Whisk in the cornflour and lemon juice until just combined. The meringue should look smooth and glossy.

3 Divide the meringue into three bowls and colour each with a couple of drops of food colour. Use a cocktail stick to add the food colouring carefully and fold the colour in using a dessert spoon. Spoon or pipe the meringue onto two baking sheets, making each one about 2½cm/1in in diameter. You will need a 13mm/½in nozzle.

4 Bake the meringues for 30 to 35 minutes until firm on the outside and the meringues release themselves from the baking paper. Turn off the oven and leave the meringues for a further 45 minutes. Remove from the oven and leave on a rack to cool. Sandwich with whipped cream or softened vanilla ice cream.

> To fill the piping bag, stand it in a tall glass and fold the edges down over the rim

A **colourful** dessert, made more yummy when sandwiched with **whipped cream**

This **snack** makes **apples** just a little more interesting and brings a smile to **reluctant fruit-eaters'** faces!

Apple Smiles
■ Makes 4 ■ Prep time: 10 mins

1 red apple, cored and sliced into eighths

A squeeze of lemon juice

Smooth peanut butter

Mini marshmallows

Spread peanut butter on one side of each apple slice (squeeze a little lemon juice over the apple if not serving immediately). Place five mini marshmallows on one apple slice and then lay another apple slice, peanut butter side down on top.

Peanut-Butter Bears

■ Serves 8 ■ Prep time: 20 mins

40g/1½oz Rice Krispies
75g/3oz icing sugar
2 tbsp sesame seeds
100g/4oz smooth peanut butter
40g/1½oz unsalted butter
16 chocolate buttons
Mini coloured sweets
Tube of black writing icing

Put the Rice Krispies in a large bowl and stir in the icing sugar and sesame seeds. Melt the peanut butter and butter in a medium pan over a low heat. Pour this over the Rice Krispies and stir with a wooden spoon until everything is well mixed together. Divide the mixture into eight and squash each portion together with your hands, then roll into a ball.

Put the balls on a baking sheet lined with baking paper. Squash down to flatten the bottoms. Push chocolate buttons into the sides for ears and place mini coloured sweets for eyes and noses. Use the writing icing to pipe pupils and mouths. Chill in the refrigerator for 30 minutes or until firm.

A fun treat that will go perfectly with a cool glass of milk

89

These easy **shortbread biscuits** are a delicious way to say 'I love you'. But if you don't have **heart-shaped cutters**, you can always use round ones. The **baked** and **sandwiched** cookies will stay fresh for up to a day if kept in an airtight container in a cool place

Shortbread Sweethearts

■ Makes 8 (easily doubled) ■ Prep time: 25 mins plus 30 mins chill time ■ Cook time: 15 mins

55g (2oz) butter, softened
30g (1oz) caster sugar
Pinch of salt
¼ tsp vanilla
85g (3oz) plain flour, plus extra for rolling

To Sandwich the Hearts
40g (1½oz) white chocolate, chopped
Icing sugar, for dusting
1 to 2 tbsp raspberry jam
(preferably seedless)

Beat together the butter, sugar, vanilla and pinch of salt. Add the flour and stir in with a wooden spoon, then bring the dough together with your hands. If the dough is very soft, wrap in clingfilm and chill for about 30 minutes.

Roll out the dough on a lightly floured surface to about 2mm (1/16in) thick. Cut out 16 heart shapes using a 6cm cookie cutter. Put eight dough hearts on one baking sheet. Cut heart centres from the remaining eight dough hearts, using a smaller cutter, and transfer to a second baking sheet. Chill both baking sheets in the freezer (10 minutes) or the refrigerator (one hour).

Preheat the oven to 180C/350F/Gas 4. Bake the shortbread until slightly golden around the edges (10 to 12 minutes for the ones with the hearts cut out and 13 to 15 minutes for the solid ones). Cool on the baking sheets for five minutes then transfer to a wire rack to cool completely.

Melt the white chocolate in a small, heat-proof bowl set over, not in, a pan of warm water. Stir frequently and watch carefully because white chocolate overheats easily. Remove the bowl from the pan when a few unmelted lumps remain and stir the mixture until smooth. Set aside for 10 to 20 minutes. Meanwhile, dust icing sugar on the cookies with the cut-out centres.

Spread ½ tbsp of white chocolate over each solid heart cookie, leaving a border around the edge (the chocolate will spread when you sandwich the cookies). Put about ¼ tsp of jam in the centre of each. Sandwich the cookies with the sugar-dusted tops and add a little extra jam in the cut-out centre if needed. Refrigerate for 10 to 20 minutes, then store in a cool place.

chilling the dough before cooking keeps the shortbread in shape when it is baked in the oven

HALLOWEEN

Ghostly cakes, bat cookies and witches' broomsticks make for a **spookily delicious** Hallowe'en party

Hallowe'en Party

Top Tips for a spooky Hallowe'en

What is it about Hallowe'en that kids find so irresistible? The excitement in our house as the sun sets on 31 October is incredible. When the clocks go back in October, it gets darker so much earlier, so Hallowe'en following so swiftly seems like a good consolation prize for the earlier evenings – and it's a great excuse for a children's party. You'll find lots of great party ideas here. A spooky atmosphere isn't spooky at all in bright sunlight, so grab your cauldron and broomstick, stick on a witch's hat and embrace the darkness!

Haunting can be hard work, and children collect all kinds of sweets and chocolate from trick or treating, so it's lovely to prepare some great home-cooked food for them to return to. Do the trick or treating early, then get everyone home to compare their booty and sit down to a filling and frightening feast.

Your children will also love getting involved in the preparation – and Hallowe'en cooking is more like sorcery: a mixing bowl is your cauldron and a wooden spoon your wand. Making the haunted food is half the fun, so encourage your wee witches and little goblins to get stuck in. Magic up eyeballs, monsters, spiders and slime together!

My inspiring Hallowe'en recipes also offer wonderful opportunities for your children to use all their senses and their imagination

Terrifying has never been so tasty

as they eat. Whether it's summoning the courage to feel a deadman's finger (p107, if you dare!), inventing crazy cake-monster adventures, peering into an orange pumpkin, sniffing slime or flapping a bat cookie around the room.

So lay out this deliciously spooky spread, dim the lights and share a ghost story or two around the table while you enjoy a devilishly delicious Hallowe'en party. Terrifying has never been so tasty!

🦇 If you want children to come trick or treating at your door, carve out a pumpkin and place a lit candle inside.

🦇 If you want to take your children trick or treating, work out a route and telephone your neighbours and friends in advance so they are not disappointed. Always have an adult accompany the children while they're out.

🦇 If you have a large pumpkin, it can be hollowed out and you can fit a glass or plastic bowl in the centre and fill it with fruit punch.

🦇 Have a basket of treats – such as wrapped sweets, bite-sized chocolate bars or some non-edible treats (novelty erasers, stickers) – to hand out to the children.

Halloween Games

Dangling Doughnuts

Tie a length of elastic or string around some ring doughnuts and hang them in a row from a pole or some string. Line up the children facing a doughnut each and tell them not to use their hands. The first one to munch through their doughnut is the winner.

Apple Bobbing

A large bowl of water is placed on the floor. The children hold their hands behind their backs and then try to lift an apple out of the water using only their teeth. Children can wear aprons if you have them and spread plenty of newspaper over the floor because this can get quite messy!

Body Parts

Only the bravest should get involved in this game! Each person plunges their hands into bowls of nasty things they can't see and guesses what they are. This is a very spooky touchy-feely game that will send shivers down the children's spines. Have several bowls and cover each one with a cloth so the children can't see what is inside.

You could use...

Lychees for eyeballs

Jelly for liver

Cauliflower for brains

Linked sausages for intestine

Wet spaghetti for veins

Oi! What are you looking at?

Your children will enjoy creating each monster's face with sweets.
Will they be **friendly** or **scary?** Let your children decide.

Scary Monster cupcakes ■ Makes 12 cakes ■ Prep time: 20 mins ■ Cook time: 20 mins

For the cupcakes

125g/4½oz soft margarine

125g/4½oz caster sugar

2 large eggs

125g/4½oz self raising flour

1 tsp vanilla essence

1 tub creamy vanilla icing

(available in large supermarkets)

For the decoration

Various food colourings

Marshmallows

Mini marshmallows

Strawberry liquorice laces

Liquorice Allsorts and

a selection of sweets

Preheat the oven to 180C/350F/Gas Mark 4. Cream the margarine and sugar together until light and fluffy, then beat in the eggs one at time, together with a tablespoon of flour. Add the vanilla essence and fold in the remaining flour.

Line a bun tin with paper cases and half fill each case with the mixture. Bake in the oven for 20 minutes. You can tell they are done when they have risen, are golden in colour and spring back into shape when pressed with your finger. Remove and cool on a wire rack.

Colour the vanilla icing using the desired food colouring. Spread the icing over the top of the cakes and have fun with your children decorating them with sweets.

use mini cupcakes to make little monster cakes

Brain cupcakes

- Makes 18
- Prep time: 20 mins
- Cook time: 20 mins

Same cupcakes as previous page
1 tub vanilla frosting
Icing sugar
Red and black food colouring

Add the icing sugar to a tub of ready-made vanilla frosting to make it stiff enough to pipe. Add a little red and black food colouring to make the brain pinkish grey. Pipe the frosting on top of the cupcakes and, using red food colouring and a cocktail stick, draw red veins on the icing.

Brains have never been so *tasty* and cupcakes have never been so clever

Ghoulish Ghost cakes

- Makes 18
- Prep time: 20 mins
- Cook time: 20 mins

175g/6oz caster sugar
175g/6oz butter
1 tsp vanilla essence
3 eggs

175g/6oz self raising flour
Cornflour
750g/1lb 6oz ready-to-roll icing
Tube of black writing icing

Preheat the oven to 180C/350F/Gas Mark 4. Beat together the caster sugar, butter and vanilla essence until light and fluffy. Add one egg at a time with a tablespoon of self raising flour for each egg. Beat well and fold in the remaining flour. Spoon into 12 greased and floured dariole moulds, to just over the halfway mark. Place on a baking tray and bake for 20 minutes. Remove from the oven and leave to cool. Cut the tops off the cakes to make flat surfaces and turn out onto a board or plate. Leave until completely cold.

Roll out the white icing on a surface dusted with cornflour and cut out 12 circles, each 15cm wide (use a saucer as a guide). Drape these over the sponge cakes to form ghost figures. From the trimmings, use a mini cutter to cut out some tiny oval shapes or roll some tiny balls of white icing into oval shapes. Dampen them with a little water and stick them onto the front of the ghost to make the eyes. Use the black writing icing to make the pupils.

People traditionally dressed up in scary costumes to ward off Hallowe'en spirits. These **ghoulish cakes** have the opposite effect on children – they can't keep away

wooh oooh!

Create a **spooky** atmosphere with these
ghost and bat cookies, then watch them get eaten

boo!

collect some twigs and hang the bats upside down from the branches

Bat and Ghost cookies

■ Makes 18 ■ Prep time: 20 mins ■ Cook time: 10 mins

For the biscuits
225g/8oz plain flour
¼ tsp salt
1 tsp baking powder
1½ tsp ground ginger
½ tsp mixed spice
50g/2oz unsalted butter
100g/4oz dark brown soft sugar
100g/4oz golden syrup
1 tbsp milk

For the icing
8g sachet dried egg white
Warm water
250g/8oz icing sugar, sifted
Black food colouring
Black and red writing icing

Preheat the oven to 180C/350F/Gas Mark 4. Sift together the flour, salt, baking powder, ginger and mixed spice. Heat the butter, sugar and golden syrup in a small pan until dissolved, stirring frequently, then allow to cool for five minutes. Stir the syrup mixture and milk into the dry ingredients. Cover with plastic film and chill for 30 minutes.

Lightly grease two baking sheets. Roll out the dough on a lightly floured surface until about 5mm/¼in thick.

Cut out ghosts, bats or other Hallowe'en shapes using cookie cutters. Use a straw to make a hole in each one if you wish to hang them later. Bake for 10 to 12 minutes until lightly browned and then cool on a wire rack.

To make the icing, mix the dried egg white to a smooth paste with a little warm water according to the packet instructions. Gradually whisk in the sifted icing sugar. Colour half of the icing black. Make a small piping bag out of greaseproof or baking paper and pipe around the outline of the biscuits and around the hole. Pipe the bat biscuits black and the ghost biscuits white. Thin out the remaining black and white icing with a little water and spread this inside the piped lines.

Once the icing has hardened, you can draw some features on the ghosts and bats using black and red writing icing. Thread some thin ribbon through the holes in the biscuits and hang them from twigs arranged in a vase.

A cross between a brownie, a muffin and a cupcake, these **yummy chocolate** confections are unlikely to hang around for long!

chocolate spider cakes

■ Makes 18 ■ Prep time: 20 mins ■ Cook time: 20 mins

For the cakes

170g/6oz dark chocolate, chopped
170g/6oz butter, cut into 2cm cubes
200g/7oz soft light brown sugar
3 eggs, at room temperature
1 tsp vanilla extract
2 tbsp sour cream
150g/5oz self raising flour
2 tbsp cocoa powder
Pinch of salt
85g/3oz milk chocolate, finely
chopped or chips (optional)

For the decoration

100g/4oz milk chocolate
Liquorice laces
16 chocolate marshmallow teacakes
Liquorice Allsorts
M&M's
Tube of writing icing

1 Preheat oven to 180C/350F/Gas Mark 4. Line two muffin tins with 16 paper cases. Put the chocolate, butter and sugar in a heatproof bowl and melt, stirring frequently. You can melt the chocolate in the microwave (about three minutes, stirring after each minute) or over a pan of warm water (make sure the base of the bowl doesn't touch the water). Set aside to cool slightly.

2 Whisk together the eggs, vanilla and sour cream. Stir this into the cooled chocolate. Into this, sift the flour, cocoa powder and salt, and fold in, along with the milk chocolate (if using).

3 Spoon into the paper cases, to about two-thirds full. Bake in the oven for 18-20 minutes, until the muffins are risen and just firm to the touch. Allow to cool for five minutes, then transfer to a cooling rack.

4 For the decoration, melt the chocolate in a heatproof bowl over a pan of simmering water. Using a palette knife, cover each cake with some of the melted chocolate. Arrange a liquorice strip for each of the spider's eight legs and stick a teacake in the centre of these. Use a blob of writing icing to stick the M&M's on to the Liquorice Allsorts for eyes.

Try using an ice cream scoop to fill the paper cases

105

Twiglet Broomsticks

■ **Prep time: 20 mins**

Grissini sticks or Sesame Seed Sticks
Mini Twiglets or pretzels
String
Chives

Attach the Mini twiglets to the Grissini sticks with some string and then tie chives around them. You may find it easier to tie them if you put the chives in the microwave for a few seconds.

Keep an eye on these **broomsticks** – they have a tendency to **fly away!**

ABOVE RECIPE & IMAGE TAKEN FROM ANNABEL KARMEL COMPLETE PARTY PLANNER//EBURY

Deadman's Finger Sandwiches

■ Serves 1   ■ Prep time: 15 mins

Thin sliced white bread, crusts removed
Soft margarine
Cream cheese
Almonds
Tomato ketchup

Gently flatten the slices of bread with a rolling pin to make them more pliable. Spread with a little margarine and some cream cheese. Roll up the sandwiches and make three indentations with a blunt knife to form the finger joints. Trim the ends of the fingers into a V shape and stick an almond on to each tip with a little cream cheese to form the nails. Now for the gruesome bit: squirt tomato ketchup over the end of each finger for the blood!

Children are intrigued by these mini versions of a carved **pumpkin**. They look **fantastic**, feel strange and taste good

Pumpkin Oranges

■ Serves 6　■ Prep time: 20 mins

6 large oranges
2 x 135g/5oz packets of jelly

Prepare the jelly according to the packet instructions, but using slightly less water so it is a little firmer, then put in the fridge to set. Cut a slice from the stalk end of each orange. Cut out eyes, a nose and a mouth shape using a sharp, pointed knife. Hollow out the oranges using a small sharp knife and spoon so that you are left with just a shell. Fill with chopped jelly.

Green Slime Lemonade

■ Serves 6　■ Prep time: 20 mins

200g/7oz caster sugar
150ml/5fl oz hot water from the kettle
6 large lemons
850ml/25fl oz still or sparkling water, chilled
Green food colouring
Slices of lime and lime zest
Orange slices
Kiwi fruit slices
Gummy sweets, such as snakes and spiders

To make the syrup, put the sugar in a heatproof bowl and add the hot water. Stir to dissolve the sugar, then set aside to cool. Roll the lemons – this helps to release the juice. Squeeze the lemons – you will need 250ml of juice. Pour the juice into a jug and stir in the sugar syrup, add the chilled water and a few drops of green food colouring. Drop in the orange and kiwi fruit slices, followed by the gummy sweets.

Homemade lemonade tastes great and it's easy to prepare. Add a few drops of food colouring to give it a more **murky** and **slimy** look...

These **warming** family recipes are designed
to keep everyone's **fire glowing**
on a chilly **winter** evening

Feast on
Bonfire Night

Feast on bonfire night

Wrap up cosily for a family trip to a fireworks display. Or enjoy a homemade dinner in the garden before waving sparklers and watching your own mini fireworks show. Food always seems to taste better when you eat it outside – whatever the weather!

Eating outside needn't be limited to summer picnics. Keep your children going with nutritious and tasty hot food, and you'll help them to get the most from the noisy excitement of bonfire night – and its inevitable late bedtime.

Seeing small faces light up in wonder as fireworks zoom and zip is wonderful. Little ones might hold your hand just a little tighter – sometimes I think they're not sure whether they should be thrilled or terrified. Half the thrill for children is simply being out in the dark in a crowd – and that's before the fireworks have even started.

Pack my sausage rolls, baby baked potatoes and toffee apples to enjoy at your local fireworks party. Or share nachos, sticky drumsticks and sausage rockets at home, while you count the rockets shooting across the sky.

A toffee apple might distract a nervous child

For all those poor souls for whom Bonfire Night is more frightening than thrilling, they can huddle together under the kitchen table with a delicious secret feast while the crashes and bangs go on above. Crunchy treats, such as nachos and toffee apples, might distract a nervous child from the noisy fireworks for a while at least. If your child does decide to hide, they'll probably find the family pets join them!

Stuffed Baked Potatoes

■ Prep time: 20 mins   ■ Cook time: 55 mins

Preheat the oven to 200C/400F/Gas Mark 6. Prick ordinary-sized potatoes (not baking potatoes) with a fork. Brush with oil and sprinkle with salt. Bake in the oven for 45 to 55 minutes or until crisp on the outside and tender inside. There are many simple toppings for baked potatoes, such as grated cheese and ham, baked beans, sliced mini sausages and flaked tuna, spring onion, sweetcorn and mayonnaise. However, if you fancy something a little different, you can try these ideas.

A baked potato is the ultimate **warming** food. Try these fresh ideas to **light up** an old favourite – perfect for a bonfire party

Mexican chicken

1 chicken breast, diced small
Generous pinch of mild chilli powder
¼ tbsp dried oregano
1 tbsp olive oil
Salt and freshly ground black pepper
½ small red onion, chopped
1 ripe tomato, diced
1½ tbsp sour cream
Tortilla chips

Mix the chicken with the chilli powder, oregano, half a tablespoon of the oil and some salt and pepper. Heat the remaining oil in a pan and sauté the onion for one minute until it begins to soften. Add the chicken and sauté for about four minutes until cooked through. Stir in the diced tomato. Cut a cross in the baked potato, spoon over the topping, add a blob of sour cream and decorate each one with a tortilla chip.

Salsa and Gruyère cheese

½ small onion, chopped
½ clove garlic crushed
½ small red pepper, diced
½ tbsp vegetable oil
200g/8oz tin chopped tomatoes
½ tbsp chopped fresh coriander or parsley
A few drops Tabasco
Salt and freshly ground black pepper
Gruyère cheese
6 tbsp sour cream

Sauté the onion, garlic and red pepper in the oil for four minutes. Add the tomatoes, coriander or parsley, Tabasco and salt and pepper, and simmer for 10 minutes. Cut the Gruyère cheese into six triangles. Cut a cross in the baked potato, spoon over the topping and put a dollop of sour cream on top. Decorate each potato with a cheese triangle for a sail.

Mexican Chicken

Salsa and Gruyère cheese

Stuffed baked potatoes are usually popular with older children, but a bit unwieldy for little ones. New potatoes make a perfect alternative for a finger-sized version

Easy to prepare in advance and refrigerate

Baby Baked Potatoes

■ Serves 4 ■ Prep time: 20 mins ■ Cook time: 45 mins

8 new potatoes (250g/8oz)

1 tsp olive oil

3 tbsp sour cream or crème fraîche

1 tbsp chopped chives or 1 small spring onion, finely chopped

30g/1oz grated cheese (optional)

Salt and freshly ground black pepper

Preheat the oven to 200C/400F/Gas Mark 6. Put the potatoes into a medium bowl, drizzle over the oil and season with a little salt and pepper. Toss to coat the potatoes with the oil then transfer to a baking sheet. Bake for 30 to 35 minutes, until the potatoes are cooked through.

Remove the potatoes from the oven and leave to cool slightly, then cut in half and carefully scoop out some of the centre with a teaspoon. Put the scooped potato into a small bowl and add the sour cream and chives. Mash together and season to taste with salt and pepper.

Spoon the filling into the potato skins and sprinkle with cheese (if using). Return to the baking sheet and bake for a further five to 10 minutes until heated through.

The filled potatoes can be refrigerated overnight, then reheated in a 200C/400F/Gas Mark 6 oven for 15 to 20 minutes.

Stuffed Sweet Potatoes with Bacon

■ Serves 6 ■ Prep time: 20 mins ■ Cook time: 1 hr

6 rashers pancetta or rindless
streaky bacon
6 medium sweet potatoes (1½kg/3lbs)
1 tbsp olive oil
4 tbsp crème fraîche or sour cream
3 spring onions, finely chopped
250g/9oz cheddar cheese, grated

Grill the pancetta or bacon until crisp. Drain on kitchen paper and crumble into small pieces. Refrigerate until needed.

Preheat the oven to 200C/400F/Gas Mark 6. Rub the skin of each potato with a little oil and put them on a baking sheet. Bake for one hour, turning over halfway through.

Remove the potatoes from the oven and leave for 15 to 20 minutes, or until cool enough to handle. Cut each potato in half, lengthways, and use a dessert spoon to carefully spoon the soft flesh into a bowl. Put the skins back on the baking sheet. Preheat the grill to high.

Mash the potato flesh with a fork or masher and stir in the crème fraîche, spring onions and half of the cheese. Spoon this filling back into the potato skins. Divide the crumbled bacon between the tops of the potatoes and sprinkle over the remaining cheese. Grill the potatoes for two to three minutes, until the cheese is bubbling.

Stuffed sweet potatoes make a nice change from ordinary potatoes and the flame-orange colour is great for an explosion-packed Bonfire Night

If you don't like bacon, just top the potatoes with cheese

Beefy Sausage Rolls

■ Serves 4 ■ Prep time: 20 mins
■ Cook time: 10 mins ■ Suitable for freezing

½ tbsp olive oil
½ small red onion, chopped
¼ tsp fresh thyme leaves
1 slice bread, crust removed
110g/4oz minced beef
1½ tbsp tomato chutney
2 tbsp grated Parmesan cheese
225g/8oz shortcrust pastry
1 egg beaten, with a pinch of salt

For parties, try cutting each roll into cocktail size

Preheat the oven to 200C/400F/Gas Mark 6. Put the oil in a small frying pan, add the onion and sauté for five minutes until soft. Stir in the thyme and set aside. Put the bread in a food processor and whizz to crumbs. Add the onion, beef, chutney and Parmesan, season with salt and pepper, and whizz again to combine.

Roll out the pastry into two rectangles, 12 x 18cm (5 x 7in) and about 2mm thick. You can collect the trimmings, re-roll and then cut into small stars using mini star-cutters. Halve the meat mixture and roll into two sausages, each 18cm long. Put one in the centre of each piece of pastry and brush the edges of the pastry with egg. Fold the edges over to enclose the meat and put the sausage rolls onto a baking sheet, seam side down. Brush one side of the stars with a little beaten egg and stick onto the roll. Brush the rolls all over with egg.

Bake for 20 to 25 minutes, until the pastry is golden brown. Check if the meat is cooked using a sharp knife. If not, return to the oven. Use a fish slice or palette knife to transfer the rolls to a cooling rack.

These tasty snack rolls are **perfect** for taking to a **firework display** to enjoy either hot or cold

117

Score the drumsticks to ensure they're cooked through

Sesame Honey Drumsticks

■ Serves 6 ■ Prep time: 10 mins ■ Cook time: 40 mins

6 chicken drumsticks
4 tbsp hoisin sauce
2 tbsp golden syrup
2 tbsp soy sauce
1 tsp veg oil
1 tbsp sesame seeds

Preheat the oven to 200C/400F/Gas Mark 6. In a non-metallic bowl, combine the hoisin sauce, golden syrup, soy sauce, oil and sesame seeds. Score the drumsticks, add to the sauce and toss well to coat. Cover and refrigerate for 30 minutes. Remove the drumsticks (keep the marinade) and place on a baking tray lined with non-stick baking paper. Brush with the marinade and cook for 40 minutes or until cooked through, basting a couple of times during this period.

Sticky Drumsticks

■ Serves 4 ■ Prep time: 10 mins ■ Cook time: 40 mins

3 tbsp plum sauce
1 tbsp soy sauce
1 tsp lemon juice
A few drops Tabasco
1 tbsp sesame seeds
4 chicken drumsticks

Mix together the plum sauce, soy sauce, lemon juice, Tabasco and sesame seeds in a bowl. Score the drumsticks several times and mix into the marinade. Leave to marinate for at least 20 minutes or overnight in the fridge. Preheat the oven to 200C/400F/Gas Mark 6. Line a baking tray or roasting tin with foil. Place the drumsticks on the tray and baste with the marinade. Roast for 35 to 40 minutes or until the chicken is cooked thoroughly, basting a few times during cooking.

Nachos with Salsa

■ Serves 8 ■ Prep time: 10 mins ■ Cook time: 2 mins

I have to make little individual plates of nachos because my children always end up arguing over who is eating the most – this is the only way I can guarantee they all get the same! However, you can just pile the tortilla chips together in the centre of the foil and scatter over the salsa and cheese, then grill and let everyone help themselves. It is also really easy to make double quantities (or more) if you need to please a crowd.

1 large tomato, skinned, deseeded and diced
1 spring onion, thinly sliced
2 tsp chopped coriander (or to taste)
1 tsp fresh lime juice
12 plain tortilla chips (30g/1oz)
30g/1oz cheddar, grated
1 tbsp sour cream
Salt and pepper

To make the salsa, mix all of the ingredients together in a bowl and season to taste with salt and pepper. Cover and chill until needed – it will keep for two days in the fridge.

To make the nachos, preheat the grill to high and line a grill tray with foil. Sit the tortilla chips on the foil and top each one with half a teaspoon of salsa and a little of the cheese. Grill for one to two minutes, until the cheese has just melted. Watch carefully because the edges of the tortilla chips tend to burn easily.

Transfer the nachos to two plates and top each one with a small blob of sour cream.

As **colourful** as real fireworks, these sausage **kebabs** will **spark interest** in all quarters

Sausage Rockets

■ Serves a party!   ■ Prep time: 5 mins   ■ Cook time: 5 mins

Cocktail sausages
Red, orange and yellow peppers
Bamboo skewers

Core and deseed the peppers and cut into triangles. Place under a hot grill until they begin to char or cook on a hot griddle brushed with oil. Thread the cooked sausages and grilled pepper triangles onto bamboo skewers.

CLOTHING COURTESY OF BODEN WWW.BODEN.CO.UK

Toffee Apples

■ **Serves 10** ■ **Prep time: 20 mins** ■ **Cook time: 10 mins**

450g/16oz demerara sugar

50g/2oz butter

2 tsp vinegar

1 tbsp golden syrup

150ml/5fl oz water

10 small apples, washed and dried

Wooden lolly sticks, or chopsticks

Put all of the ingredients for the toffee coating in a heavy-based saucepan. Heat gently, stirring all the time, until the sugar has dissolved. Bring to the boil and boil rapidly, without stirring, until the temperature reaches 143C/290F on a sugar thermometer. If you don't have a thermometer, drop a little of the hot syrup into cold water – the coating is ready when it separates into hard threads.

Before covering the apples, push thick wooden chopsticks into them. Then, dip them carefully into the hot toffee mixture, swirling them around and allowing the excess to drip off so the coating is not too thick. Leave to set on wax paper or greased aluminium foil.

World Taste Tour

Take your child's tastebuds on a **world tour**
to discover **deliciously different**
flavours and exciting new ways to eat

World Taste Tour

It's easy to fall into cooking habits and stick with old favourites that always work. But injecting fresh flavours, colours and textures into the mix really is inspiring. So let's celebrate the delicious diversity of the world and its fabulous cuisines.

Your family can enjoy what the world has to offer with no airport queues, no plane delays and no hassle. These imaginative recipes bring the tastes of the globe to you. Of course, I can't guarantee these dishes won't make you yearn for an exotic family holiday next year – they certainly provoke long-distance yearnings in my family.

World cuisine is about more than cooking: for example, you could turn an everyday family dinner into a Chinese banquet. Serve food in little bowls and help your child to give chopsticks a try. Either use special kids' ones or fold a piece of paper into a small square and use an elastic band to secure it at the top to make regular chopsticks into pincers – much easier for little hands.

Children are creatures of habit, so to help them take the brave leap into new food territory, these recipes start with winning ingredients, such as chicken and salmon. If your child is pasta-mad, try my Singapore

Noodles (p135), a refreshing change from spaghetti and tomato sauce – and why leave fruity flavours, such as mango and coconut, for dessert? My family can't get enough of my Fruity Chicken Curry (p127); perfect for a relaxed family supper. Dim Sum can be lots of fun too. Children love peeking inside the Moneybag Wontons (p128) to see what delicious surprises are packed within the tiny, paper-thin parcels.

Offering your child new flavours can help to stave off fussy eating. Getting used to

Take the brave leap into new food territory

different textures, colours and smells in food will help your child feel eager, rather than anxious, about eating on holiday or at friends' houses. Introducing some of your favourite cuisines, such as Indian, Chinese and Thai, at home also means you can feel confident about trying local restaurants together.

So give these recipes a go and plan a lovely family evening out!

Sesame Beef Stir-Fry

■ Serves 4 ■ Prep time: 10 mins
■ Cook time: 15 mins ■ Suitable for freezing

1 tbsp sesame oil
1 clove garlic, crushed
1 medium carrot, cut into matchsticks
100g/4oz baby sweetcorn, cut into quarters
1 courgette, cut into matchsticks
300g/10oz beef fillet, cut into very fine strips
1 tbsp cornflour
150ml/5fl oz beef stock
2 tbsp dark brown sugar
2 tbsp soy sauce
A few drops of Tabasco sauce
1 tbsp sesame seeds

It is important to include red meat in your child's diet because it provides the richest source of iron – and iron deficiency is the most common nutritional deficiency in children in the UK. When your iron stores are low, less of the oxygen carrying haemoglobin is made and less oxygen gets to the brain, resulting in difficulty concentrating and a shortened attention span. A lack of iron also makes you feel tired.

Stir-fries take so little time to cook. This nutrient-packed meal can be ready in just a few minutes

Heat the sesame oil in a wok and stir-fry the garlic and vegetables for three to four minutes. Add the beef and continue to stir-fry for four to five minutes. Mix the cornflour with a tablespoon of water and stir into the beef stock. Stir this into the pan, with the sugar, soy sauce, Tabasco and sesame seeds. Simmer until slightly thickened. Serve with rice.

This is a favourite with my family – simple to make, with a deliciously mild, fruity flavour

This is great served with poppadums and fluffy white rice

Fruity chicken curry

■ Serves 2 ■ Prep time: 10 mins ■ Cook time: 20 mins ■ Suitable for freezing

2 tbsp vegetable oil

1 onion, peeled and chopped

1 small carrot, cut into matchsticks

1 clove garlic, crushed

1 medium apple, peeled and thinly sliced

2 chicken breasts (350g/12oz), cut into bite-sized chunks

1 tbsp korma curry paste

½ tbsp mango chutney

1 tbsp tomato purée

100g/4oz frozen peas

150ml/5fl oz coconut milk

1 chicken stock cube, dissolved in

150 ml/5fl oz boiling water

Salt and freshly ground black pepper

Heat the oil in a wok or frying pan and sauté the onion and carrot for three minutes. Add the garlic and sauté for half a minute. Add the apple and stir-fry for three minutes. Add the chicken and stir-fry for four minutes.

Add the korma curry paste, mango chutney, tomato purée, coconut milk and chicken stock, and simmer for about 10 minutes. Season to taste. Four minutes before the end of the cooking time, add the frozen peas. Do not turn up the heat or the chicken will become tough and stringy.

Add more curry paste if you want a hotter dish!

Moneybag Wontons Dim Sum

■ Makes 12　■ Prep time: 25 mins　■ Cook time: 8 mins　■ Suitable for freezing

For the wontons

30g/1oz baby spinach leaves, washed
110g/4oz raw prawns
4 water chestnuts, quartered
2 spring onions, thinly sliced
1 tsp grated fresh ginger
1 tsp mirin
1 tsp sugar
1 tsp oyster sauce
½ tsp soy sauce
12 wonton wrappers

For the dipping sauce

1 tbsp soy sauce
1 tbsp water
2 tsp rice wine vinegar
1 tbsp soft light brown sugar
½ tsp toasted sesame oil
¼ tsp grated ginger

You will also need

A steamer basket and pan
Baking paper

Put a tablespoon of water in a medium saucepan and heat until steaming. Add the spinach, cover and cook for one to two minutes, until the spinach has wilted. Drain and allow to cool slightly, and then squeeze out as much liquid as possible. Transfer the spinach to a food processor, add the water chestnuts and whizz briefly, until chopped. Add the prawns, onions, ginger, mirin, sugar, oyster sauce and soy sauce, and pulse seven to eight times, until the prawns are roughly chopped.

Lay a wonton on a chopping board and dampen the edges (use a brush or a finger dipped in water). Put two teaspoons of the filling in the centre of the wonton and bring the corners together. Pinch just above the filling to seal. Sit the wonton on a baking sheet lined with clingfilm and cover with another piece of clingfilm. Repeat with the remaining wonton wrappers and filling. Put them in the fridge for a couple of hours.

For the dipping sauce, stir all the ingredients together until the sugar has dissolved.

To cook the wontons, line the base of a steamer basket with a circle of non-stick baking paper (the Chinese often use lettuce leaves) and sit the wontons on the parchment. Place the steamer basket over a pot of boiling water and cover. Steam for eight minutes, until cooked all the way through. Serve with extra soy sauce for dipping.

To freeze: cover the wontons on a tray and place in freezer for two to three hours, until solid. Transfer to a plastic freezer bag and store in the freezer for up to one month. Steam direct from frozen and increase steaming time to 10 minutes.

Mirin is a sweet Japanese cooking wine and is available in large supermarkets

Chicken and Prawn Dumplings Dim Sum

■ Makes 10　■ Prep time: 25 mins　■ Cook time: 8 mins　■ Suitable for freezing

For the dumplings

125g/5oz minced chicken or pork
125g/5oz peeled raw tiger prawns
(deveined and roughly diced)
1 large spring onion, finely chopped
¼ tsp grated root ginger
1 tbsp soy sauce
1 tbsp sake
1 tsp sesame oil
2 tsp cornflour
10 wonton wrappers

For the dipping sauce

1 tbsp soy sauce
1 tbsp water
2 tsp rice wine vinegar
1 tbsp soft light brown sugar
½ tsp toasted sesame oil
¼ tsp grated ginger

Put all the ingredients for the filling into a bowl and mix together. Lay a wonton wrapper on a chopping board. Put two teaspoons of the filling in the centre of the wonton, then gather up the sides of the wonton wrapper and mould around the filling, leaving the centre exposed. Sit the wonton on a baking sheet lined with clingfilm, and cover with another piece of clingfilm. Repeat with the remaining wonton wrappers and filling.

Oil the bottom of a bamboo steamer or stainless steel steamer and line with greaseproof paper. Put the dumplings in the steamer, cover with a lid and place over a pan of boiling water, making sure the water does not touch the base of the steamer. Steam the dumplings for 6 to 8 minutes until cooked.

For the dipping sauce, stir all the ingredients together until the sugar has dissolved.
To freeze the dumplings, follow the same instructions as above recipe.

Wontons make great finger food and are surprisingly easy to make at home – and children will enjoy helping to assemble the little parcels

I love taking my family for **dim sum**. Children love peeking inside the **steamer baskets** to see what tasty morsels are inside

Laksa comes from Singapore and Malaysia, where 'slurping' your noodles is considered essential!

corn and chicken Laksa

■ Serves 4 ■ Prep time: 10 mins ■ Cook time: 15 mins ■ Suitable for freezing

110g/4oz noodles (vermicelli preferred, but medium pad thai noodles are fine)
1 small onion, finely chopped
1 clove garlic, crushed
1 tbsp mild curry paste
1 tbsp soft light brown sugar
400ml/14fl oz coconut milk
250ml/9fl oz chicken stock
2 tsp soy sauce
200g/7oz tin sweetcorn or frozen corn kernels

60g/2oz frozen peas
110g/4oz cooked chicken, shredded
4 spring onions, thinly sliced, plus 2 extra to serve (optional)
2 tsp lime juice
2 tsp sunflower oil

Optional
Handful coriander leaves
Thinly sliced red chilli
Extra lime quarters

Cook the noodles according to packet instructions. Drain and divide between four bowls. Sauté the onion in the sunflower oil for five to six minutes, until soft. Add the garlic, curry paste and sugar, and cook for a further minute. Add the coconut milk, chicken stock and soy sauce, bring to the boil and then drop in the sweetcorn kernels, frozen peas, chicken and spring onions. Simmer for three minutes, until everything is hot, then remove from the heat and add the lime juice. Ladle the soup over the noodles and eat straight away. You can put out bowls of coriander leaves, extra spring onions, sliced chilli and lime quarters so everyone can help themselves to their favourites.

Lime wedges will add a nice twist to this spicy laksa

This is a **tasty** way to get your child to eat more **oily fish**. The **Omega 3** essential fatty acids are great for them

Teryaki Salmon and Easy chinese Fried Rice

■ Serves 4　■ Prep time: 15 mins　■ Cook time: 22 mins

For the salmon

1 tbsp sesame seeds

200g/7oz skinless boneless salmon fillet

Small piece of ginger

1 tbsp runny honey

1½ tsp soy sauce

For the rice

200g/7oz basmati rice

65g/2½oz carrots, finely chopped

75g/3oz frozen peas

5ml/1 tsp vegetable oil

1 egg, lightly beaten

25g/1oz butter

65g/2½oz onion, finely chopped

2 tbsp soy sauce

1 spring onion, finely sliced

Salt and freshly ground black pepper

Soak six wooden skewers in cold water for 30 minutes. Meanwhile, toast sesame seeds in a small frying pan over a medium heat for two to three minutes, stirring two or three times. Spread out on a plate and allow to cool.

Wash your hands. Preheat the grill to high. Cut the salmon into 1cm/½in cubes. Thread three to four onto each skewer and lay the skewers, in one layer, on a foil-lined baking tray.

For the teriyaki sauce, scrape the skin from the ginger using the tip of a teaspoon, and grate it finely. You need a quarter of a teaspoon. Put it in a bowl with the honey (rub a little oil on the spoon to make the honey slide off more easily when measuring) and soy sauce, and mix together.

Brush some of the teriyaki sauce onto the salmon and grill for two minutes, as close to the heat as possible. Brush again with the teriyaki sauce and grill for another two minutes. Turn the skewers over and repeat the brushing and grilling process. Sprinkle sesame seeds over the salmon before serving.

Cook the rice in a pan of lightly salted, boiling water, together with the chopped carrots, according to the instructions on the packet. Four minutes before the end of the cooking time, add the frozen peas. Meanwhile, heat the vegetable oil in a frying pan or wok. Beat the egg together with a little salt, tilt the pan so the egg coats the base and cook until it's set as a thin omelette. Remove from the pan, roll up and cut into thin strips.

Add the butter to the wok and sauté the onion for two minutes. Add the cooked rice mixture, the soy sauce and a little freshly ground black pepper. Stir-fry the rice for about two minutes. Stir in the strips of egg and spring onion, and heat through.

Annabel's Thai Chicken Soup

■ Serves 4 ■ Prep time: 10 mins ■ Cook time: 10 mins ■ Suitable for freezing

1 tbsp light olive oil

150g/5oz chopped onion

1 clove garlic, crushed

½ red chilli, finely chopped

1 chicken breast, cut into thin strips

100g/4oz broccoli

600ml/20fl oz chicken stock

300ml/10fl oz coconut milk

Salt and freshly ground black pepper

150g/5oz cooked rice (40g uncooked)

Heat the oil in a pan and sauté the onion, garlic and chilli for two minutes. Add the strips of chicken and sauté for two more minutes. Cut the broccoli into small florets. Add these and the chicken stock to the pan, bring to the boil and then simmer for three to four minutes. Stir in the coconut milk and simmer for a further two minutes. Season to taste, stir in the cooked rice and heat through.

Singapore Noodles

■ Serves 4　■ Prep time: 12 mins plus 30 mins marinating　■ Cook time: 15 mins　■ Suitable for freezing

For the noodles

150g/5oz chicken breast fillet

2½ tbsp vegetable oil

1 beaten egg

1 garlic clove, peeled and chopped

¼ tsp red chilli, finely chopped (optional)

75g/2½oz baby sweetcorn

75g/2½oz each carrots and courgettes,
cut into thin strips

75g/2½oz beansprouts

½ tbsp mild curry powder

4 tbsp strong chicken stock

90g/3oz small peeled prawns

3 spring onions, thinly sliced

150g/5oz Chinese noodles

For the marinade

1 tsp each of soy sauce and sake

½ tsp sugar

1 tsp cornflour

Mix the marinade ingredients in a bowl, cut the chicken into thin strips, add to the bowl and marinate for at least 30 minutes.

Heat half a tablespoon of oil in a frying pan, add the egg and fry to make a thin omelette. Remove from the pan and cut into ribbons. Heat a tablespoon of oil in a wok and sauté the garlic (and chilli, if using) for 30 seconds. Drain the chicken, add to the pan and cook for three to four minutes, then set aside. Heat the remaining oil in the wok. Add the baby sweetcorn and carrots, and stir-fry for two minutes. Add the courgettes and beansprouts, and cook for two minutes. Stir the curry powder into the stock and add to the wok. Return the chicken to the wok with the prawns, spring onions and egg, and fry for two minutes.

Cook the noodles in boiling, lightly salted water according to the instructions on the packet. Drain, mix with the stir-fry and heat through.

If you prefer, replace the **prawns** with pork or more chicken. For **extra flavour**, fry the beaten egg in half a tablespoon of sesame oil

135

Paella originates from the region of Valencia in **Spain** and gets its name from the pan it is cooked in – a **paellera**!

Annabel's Paella

■ Serves 4　■ Prep time: 10 mins　■ Cook time: 23 mins　■ Suitable for freezing

200g/7oz long-grain rice
1 tbsp olive oil
1 onion, finely chopped
1 clove garlic, crushed
1 tsp smoked paprika or sweet paprika
½ red pepper, diced
200g/7oz tin chopped tomatoes

650ml/22fl oz chicken stock
1 tbsp tomato purée
170g/6oz cooked prawns
170g/6oz cooked chicken
55g/2oz frozen peas
Handful parsley leaves, chopped

Put the rice in a colander and rinse well under cold running water. Leave to drain. Heat the oil in a large non-stick frying pan or wok and sauté the onion for five minutes, until soft. Add the garlic, paprika, pepper and rice, and cook for three minutes, stirring constantly. Pour in the chopped tomatoes, stock and tomato purée. Sweet smoked paprika is available in some supermarkets and Spanish delicatessens, and also online from www.delicioso.co.uk. Keep a tin in your kitchen because it adds a wonderful flavour to recipes.

Simmer for about 15 minutes, until the rice is tender and the stock has been absorbed. While the rice is cooking, shred the chicken into small pieces and roughly chop the parsley leaves. Stir the chicken, prawns and peas into the paella, and cook for a further two minutes, until everything is hot. Scatter with chopped parsley and serve.

This is a great way to use up leftover chicken or prawns

chicken Fajitas

■ Serves 2 ■ Prep time: 12 mins ■ Cook time: 8 mins

you can replace the chicken with beef strips

Mexican food is surprisingly **popular** with children – they like **fajitas** because they can eat them with their fingers

2 tsp tomato ketchup
1 tsp balsamic vinegar
1 tsp water
½ tsp brown sugar
Pinch dried oregano
2 drops Tabasco (optional)
1 tsp sunflower oil
1 chicken breast, sliced into thin strips
1 medium red onion, thinly sliced
¼ small red pepper, thinly sliced
¼ small yellow pepper, thinly sliced
2 flour tortillas

2 tbsp mild salsa (use recipe below or a shop-bought salsa)
4 tsp sour cream
1 tbsp guacamole (optional)

For the mild salsa
1 large tomato, skinned, deseeded and diced
1 spring onion, thinly sliced
2 tsp chopped coriander (or to taste)
1 tsp fresh lime juice
Salt and freshly ground black pepper

Mix the ketchup, balsamic vinegar, water, sugar, oregano and Tabasco (if using) in a small bowl and set aside. Heat the oil in a large pan or wok and stir-fry the chicken for two minutes. Add the vegetables and stir-fry for a further three to four minutes, until the chicken has cooked through and the vegetables have softened slightly. Add the ketchup mixture and cook, stirring for a further minute, and remove from the heat.

To make the salsa, mix all of the ingredients in a small bowl and season to taste with salt and pepper. Alternatively, use a mild shop-bought salsa. Cover and chill until needed – it will keep for up to two days in the fridge.

Warm the tortillas for 10 to 15 seconds in a microwave or for one minute each in a dry frying pan. Spoon the fajita filling down the centre of the wrap and spoon over the salsa, sour cream and guacamole (if using). Roll up and serve immediately.

Any leftover filling will keep, covered, in the fridge for up to two days. Reheat for about a minute in a microwave, until piping hot.

Delicious Christmas

Fill your home with the warming aroma of Christmas baking and create your own festive family traditions

Delicious Christmas

Remember when Christmas took forever to come? Now, it's here before we know it! Little ones are full of excitable festive spirit as soon as December starts. With schools and nurseries finishing well before Father Christmas visits, cooking lovely festive goodies together is a great way of channelling your child's eager anticipation.

Christmas is the best time to be at home

Christmas is the best time of the year to be at home. Outside, it's just short days, wet weather and shopping mayhem – and because there seems to be so much to buy, creating decorations with your child is an easy and enjoyable antidote to the consumer madness. Use ribbon to tie my Stained Glass Window Cookies (p145) to your Christmas tree – they look gorgeous with the glow of fairy lights shining through. Or try hanging them by your windows to catch the light. Tie them high if little hands and paws get too tempted.

Giving homemade gifts is really special. Children feel so proud and happy to give friends, family or teachers something they've made themselves. Try my Peppermint and Rose Kisses (p151), Christmas Pudding

Truffles (p157) or one of my Christmas cookie recipes (p147 and p153) – they look great and taste even better. You can put them in cellophane bags tied with ribbon or place them in small cardboard boxes – but wrap them up quickly before the little cooks help them to disappear!

Keeping food simple and warming makes Christmas parties easy and fun. Try Rudolph the Red-Nosed Baked Potatoes (p159) to delight visiting children and blow their minds with Snazzy Snowmen (p154) for dessert. Share my Turkey Meatballs and Spaghetti (p158) for a nourishing family supper with a festive flavour.

Traditional Christmas dinner can be a bit overwhelming for little eyes and tiny tummies. My Mini Turkey and Potato Pies (p161) are a lifesaver on a busy Christmas morning because you can make them beforehand. They're perfect for giving your child their own special Christmas dinner – one you know they'll enjoy, so you can sit down, relax and have your own well-earned Christmas too.

Wishing you a very merry and truly tasty Christmas!

Annabel Karmel

Whatever the occasion and whatever their age Annabel Karmel has the perfect recipe

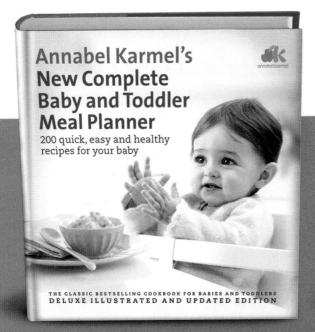

Annabel Karmel's New Complete Baby and Toddler Meal Planner
200 quick, easy and healthy recipes for your baby

THE CLASSIC BESTSELLING COOKBOOK FOR BABIES AND TODDLERS
DELUXE ILLUSTRATED AND UPDATED EDITION

Annabel Karmel princess party cookbook
over 100 delicious recipes and fun ideas

From the bestselling author
The New Complete Baby and Toddler Meal Planner

NEW

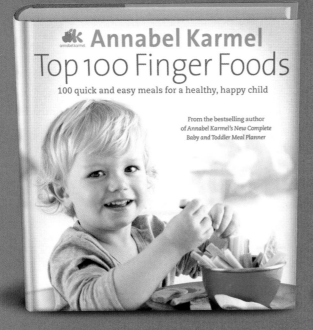

Annabel Karmel Top 100 Finger Foods
100 quick and easy meals for a healthy, happy child

From the bestselling author of Annabel Karmel's New Complete Baby and Toddler Meal Planner

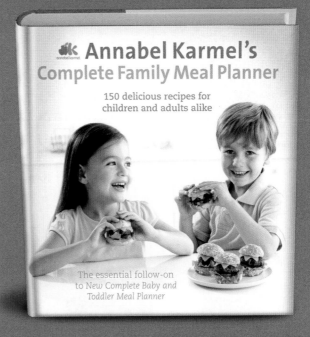

Annabel Karmel's Complete Family Meal Planner
150 delicious recipes for children and adults alike

The essential follow-on to New Complete Baby and Toddler Meal Planner

2.5 MILLION BOOKS SOLD

EBURY PRESS Ebury Press is an imprint of Ebury Publishing, A Random House Company / www.rbooks.co.uk

www.ANNABELKARMEL.com

These novelty cookies – shaped like stars, Christmas trees and angels – are fun to make. Children enjoy crushing the sweets and using cookie cutters to make the shapes from dough

144

Stained-Glass Window Cookies

■ Makes 25 ■ Prep time: 50 mins ■ Cook time: 12 mins

350g/12oz plain flour
1 tsp bicarbonate of soda
2 tsp ground ginger
½ tsp salt
100g/4oz butter

175g/6oz soft brown sugar
1 egg
4 tbsp golden syrup
Different coloured fruit-flavoured
boiled sweets
Narrow ribbon

1 Preheat oven to 180C/350F/Gas Mark 4. Mix the flour, bicarbonate of soda, ginger and salt in a bowl. Rub in the butter until the mixture resembles fine breadcrumbs and then stir in the sugar. Beat together the egg and golden syrup and mix into the flour mixture to make a smooth dough, kneading lightly with your hands.

2 Crush the sweets in their wrappers using a rolling pin. Sprinkle flour on a clean work surface and roll out the dough until about ½cm/¼in thick,

3 Cut the dough into shapes using a selection of Christmas cookie cutters. Transfer to lined baking sheets.

4 Cut out shapes in the centre of each biscuit, making sure you leave a good edge all the way around the biscuit.

5 Fill the hole in each biscuit with crushed boiled sweets. Make a hole at the top of each biscuit using a drinking straw so you will be able to thread a ribbon through it later. Bake for 11 to 12 minutes until golden.

Make a hole in each one with a drinking straw then thread with ribbon and hang

These **warming**, spiced snowflake biscuits look lovely hung on the Christmas tree. Use white icing for a **fresh and frosty** effect

Ginger and Spice Snowflake Cookies

■ Makes 15 ■ Prep time: 45 mins ■ Cook time: 12 mins ■ Suitable for freezing (undecorated)

225g/8oz plain flour
¼ tsp salt
1 tsp baking powder
1½ tsp ground ginger
½ tsp mixed spice
1 egg yolk, lightly beaten
50g/2oz unsalted butter
100g/4oz dark brown soft sugar
100g/4oz golden syrup
1 tbsp milk
White decorating sugar for sprinkling
Tube of white writing icing

Sift together the flour, salt, baking powder, ginger and mixed spice. Heat the butter, brown sugar and golden syrup in a small pan, stirring frequently until dissolved, then allow to cool for five minutes. Stir the syrup mixture, egg yolk and milk into the dry ingredients and form into a ball of dough. Cover with plastic film and chill for 30 minutes.

Preheat the oven to 180C/350F/Gas Mark 4. Roll out the dough on a lightly floured work surface until about 5mm/¼in thick. Cut into snowflakes using snowflake-shaped cutters and arrange these on baking sheets that have been lined with baking paper. Use mini cutters to create the intricate snowflake detail (for easy release, spray the inside of the cutters with cooking spray).

Bake the biscuits for 11 to 12 minutes or until golden. Allow them to cool on the baking tray for five minutes and then transfer them to a wire rack to cool completely.

Empty the tube of white writing icing into an icing bag and pipe designs onto the snowflakes. Sprinkle with decorating sugar. Thread a thin ribbon around the cookies and hang them on the Christmas tree or store them in an airtight tin until read to eat.

This **delicious granola** is very versatile. Have it for **breakfast** with milk, on its own as a **snack** or layered with yoghurt, honey and fruit

Annabel's Granola

■ Makes 6 to 8   ■ Prep time: 5 mins   ■ Cook time: 45 mins

175g/6oz rolled oats
70g/2½oz coarsely chopped pecans
20g/1oz shredded/desiccated coconut
¼ tsp salt
120g/4½oz soft brown sugar
2 tbsp canola or sunflower oil
4 tbsp maple syrup
25g/1oz raisins
25g/1oz cranberries

Preheat oven to 150C/300F/Gas Mark 2. Mix the oats, nuts, coconut, salt and sugar. Whisk the oil and syrup together, and mix well with the oats. Spread on a lightly oiled baking sheet and bake for 40 to 45 minutes, stirring every 10 minutes. Put in a bowl, stir in the fruit and leave to cool.

Wholegrain cereals are a good source of iron. To help your child absorb it, give them vitamin C-rich fruit, such as kiwi, or vitamin C-rich juice, such as orange or cranberry

Try dipping one half of the peppermint cream in melted dark chocolate

These beautiful **fondant creams** don't need to be baked, so your **child can help** to make them from start to finish

These colourful peppermint creams will make a lovely gift for friends

Peppermint and Rose Kisses ■ Makes 32 ■ Prep time: 35 mins

1 egg white
340g/12oz icing sugar
6 to 7 drops peppermint flavouring
Green food colouring
Pink food colouring
1 tbsp rosewater

Lightly whisk the egg white until frothy and sift in the icing sugar. Stir thoroughly with a wooden spoon until the mixture is quite stiff. Knead with your hands on a clean work surface, dusted with icing sugar, and divide into two balls. Knead the peppermint essence and a few drops of green food colouring into one ball, and the rosewater and a few drops of pink food colouring into the other.

Roll the mixture into small balls and place these on a lined baking sheet. Flatten them with a fork and then leave them to set for 24 hours. If you have decorative stamps, you can make these creams even prettier.

cranberries are a great antioxidant

These delicious cookies are very quick and easy to make. Take them out of the oven when they're quite soft so, when they cool down, they are crisp on the outside, but moist inside

White Chocolate and Cranberry Cookies

■ Makes 30 ■ Prep time: 15 mins ■ Cook time: 12 mins ■ Suitable for freezing

For the cookies
100g/4oz softened unsalted butter
100g/4oz golden caster sugar
100g/4oz light muscovado sugar
1 egg
1 tsp vanilla essence
175g/6oz plain flour
½ tsp baking powder
¼ tsp salt
150g/5oz white chocolate, cut into small chunks
75g/3oz dried cranberries

For the buttercream filling
75g/3oz butter, softened
125g/4½oz icing sugar, sifted
A few drops vanilla essence
2 tsp milk

Preheat oven to 190C/375F/Gas Mark 5. Beat the butter together with the sugars. Use a fork to beat the egg together with the vanilla essence and add this to the butter mixture. In a bowl, mix together the flour, baking powder and salt, add this to the butter and egg mixture, and blend well. Mix in the chunks of white chocolate and cranberries.

To make the cookies, line four baking sheets with non-stick baking paper. Form the dough into walnut-sized balls and arrange on the baking sheets, spaced well apart. Bake in the oven for 12 minutes. Allow them to cool for a few minutes and then transfer to a wire rack.

To make the buttercream for the filling, beat the softened butter until creamy. Sift the icing sugar into the bowl and beat together with the butter. Finally, beat in the vanilla and milk. Spread the buttercream over one of the cookies and place a second cookie on top.

These are **fun** for
children to make
themselves. You can line boxes
or tins with shredded cellophane
or some tissue paper and
nestle your **decorated**
cakes inside

Put the fizzy lances in
the microwave for a
few seconds to make
them more pliable

Snazzy Snowmen

■ Makes 8 to 10　■ Prep time: 35 mins　■ Cook time: 20 mins

100g/4oz softened butter or soft
margarine
100g/4oz golden caster sugar
2 eggs
100g/4oz self raising flour
1 tsp baking powder
1 tsp vanilla essence
Icing sugar for dusting
150g/5oz ready-to-roll white icing
3 tbsp apricot jam
Marshmallows
Red fizzy lances for the scarves
Tubes of coloured writing icing
Sugar baubles (for cake decoration) and
edible silver baubles

Preheat the oven to 180C/300F/Gas Mark 2. Place the softened butter or margarine, sugar, eggs, flour, baking powder and vanilla essence into the bowl of an electric mixer. Beat for a few minutes until the mixture is light in colour and fluffy.

Line a bun tin with eight paper cases and divide the mixture between them, filling the cases to about two-thirds of the way up. Bake for about 20 minutes until the fairy cakes have risen and are lightly golden. Lift the cakes (still in their paper cases) out of the tins and leave them to cool on a wire rack.

Dust a clean work surface with icing sugar and roll out the icing to about 5mm/¼in thick. Cut out eight circles using a small pastry cutter that is the same size as the top of your cakes. Put the apricot jam into a small dish and stir in one tablespoon of hot water. Brush this over the surface of the cakes and stick the circles of icing on top.

To decorate the cakes, use marshmallows for the snowmen's heads, black writing icing for the eyes, red writing icing for the smiles and sugar baubles for noses (stick them on with a blob of writing icing). Stick the heads on the cakes using a little apricot jam, then stick on the edible silver baubles for buttons. Wrap fizzy lances around the snowmen's necks for scarves.

Father Christmas Carrot Cupcakes

■ Makes 16　■ Prep time: 35 mins　■ Cook time: 22 mins　■ Suitable for freezing (before icing)

For the cupcakes
170g/6oz self raising flour
½ tsp bicarbonate of soda
1 tsp mixed spice
Pinch of salt
170g/6oz butter, room temperature
170g/6oz soft light brown sugar
3 eggs, beaten
½ tsp vanilla extract
2 tbsp sour cream or Greek yoghurt
140g/5oz grated carrot (2 large or 3 medium carrots)
110g/4oz raisins
Small chocolate honeycomb balls/chips

For the Father Christmas decoration
225g/8oz ready-to-roll white white icing
3 tbsp apricot jam
Chocolate honeycomb balls
Red food colouring
White writing icing

For the Maple icing
140g/5oz icing sugar
4 tbsp maple syrup
¾ tbsp water
30g/1oz pecan nuts, chopped (optional)

Preheat the oven to 190C /375F/Gas Mark 5. Line two bun tins with paper cases. Sift together the flour, bicarbonate of soda, mixed spice and salt, and set aside. Put the butter and sugar in a large bowl and beat until fluffy. Add the eggs, vanilla, sour cream and sifted dry ingredients, and beat until just combined. Fold in the carrot and raisins.

Spoon the batter into the prepared bun tins, filling each paper case around three-quarters full. Bake for 18 to 22 minutes, until a toothpick inserted into the centre of the cupcakes comes out clean. Cool for five minutes in the tins, then transfer to a wire rack to cool completely.

To make Father Christmas faces, colour one third of the icing red. Roll out some of the white icing and cut out circles to fit the cupcakes. Warm the apricot jam in a small saucepan and brush a little over the surface of the cakes. Place the circles of white icing on top. Cut out triangles to form hats from the red icing and attach a small white ball of icing at the top of the hat for a bobble. Add two chocolate honeycomb balls or chocolate chips for the eyes and use the tube of writing icing to make a beard and hair on each face.

To make the maple icing (if you choose not to decorate these as Father Christmas), put the icing sugar in a bowl and stir in the maple syrup. Add the water, a few drops at a time, to make an icing that will thickly coat the back of a spoon. Spread onto the cupcakes and sprinkle over the pecans (if using).

The iced cupcakes will keep in an airtight tin for three to four days. Baked, un-iced cupcakes can be frozen for up to a month. Defrost for two to three hours at room temperature.

These **carrot cupcakes** are also delicious when simply topped with maple icing

www.dk.com

Annabel's
expert advice
on how to cook **for**
and **with** your children

annabel karmel

www.annabelkarmel.com